Caregiving Fathers in the Workplace

Jasmine Kelland

Caregiving Fathers in the Workplace

Organisational Experiences and the Fatherhood
Forfeit

Jasmine Kelland
Plymouth Business School
University of Plymouth
Plymouth, UK

ISBN 978-3-030-97970-6   ISBN 978-3-030-97971-3   (eBook)
https://doi.org/10.1007/978-3-030-97971-3

This Palgrave Macmillan imprint is published by the registered company Springer Nature Switzerland AG.
The registered company address is: Gewerbestrasse 11, 6330 Cham, Switzerland

This book is dedicated to Roger Spry and Rosemarie Kelland—I admired you both so very much.

Acknowledgements

I would like to take this opportunity to acknowledge the many of the individuals who have helped with this research.

Firstly, I would like to thank all of the participants, for being so open with your views, sharing your experiences and giving up your very precious time to take part in this research.

Secondly, I'd like to acknowledge my University of Plymouth colleagues who helped me with the development of this work, particularly Professor Duncan Lewis whose guidance (and patience!) was invaluable.

Thirdly, to my nieces, nephews and god children, Amelia and Max; Sienna and Oliver; Lucie; Isaac and Jacup; Sienna, Asher and Isaac; Amelia and Ethan; Felix and Imogen; Bethany, Lauren, James and Holly—your parents are truly amazing, watching them navigate caregiving and work so effectively on a daily basis was an inspiration to this book.

Fourthly, a huge thank-you goes to my family, Chris, Grace, Lois and Felicity—so much work went into this research and their support and encouragement can never be underestimated. Also, my parents and my parents-in-law for all of the reassurance and childminding whilst I wrote a book about caregiving and for not laughing at the irony. I am so lucky to have you all.

Finally, I would like to acknowledge my late grandfather, Roger Spry—he was the biggest advocate for this research by a country mile; despite being born in 1930 his views on the importance of egalitarian parenting were steadfast.

CONTENTS

ABOUT THE AUTHOR

Jasmine Kelland is Lecturer in Human Resource Management and a Programme Leader at the University of Plymouth. Prior to joining academia she had a successful career in Human Resources, working in HR Management in various organisations such as the NHS, Boots the Chemist and ITV.

Dr Kelland's work on the 'fatherhood forfeit' has been widely cited within the press (such as *The Guardian*, *The Independent* and *New Scientist*), by professional bodies (such as CIPD), and she has contributed to numerous blogs and webinars on the topic of fathers at work. Her 'fatherhood forfeit' research has been published by the House of Commons Women and Equalities Select Committee and referred to in a House of Commons debate exploring 'Fathers in the Family'. She has presented her research to the UK Parliament All-Party Parliamentary Group on Fatherhood, professional and international academic conferences, and numerous organisations. Additionally, she has discussed the challenges facing caregiving fathers through media outlets such as Sky News and BBC Radio.

She lives in Devon with her husband and three daughters.

CHAPTER 1

Introduction

Abstract

Modern families face a range of challenges as they seek the right balance between working and family life. … Just as mothers have sought equality in access to employment, fathers increasingly want to combine work with time spent fulfilling childcare responsibilities. (House of Commons Women and Equalities Select Committee, 2017)

It has been widely acknowledged within existing literature that there are numerous benefits to both children and parents to fathers taking an active role in the caregiving of their children (Levtov et al., *State of the world's fathers: A MenCare advocacy publication*. Promundo, Rutgers, Save the Children, Sonke Gender Justice, and the MenEngage Alliance, 2015; Burgess & Davies, *Cash or carry? Fathers combining work and care in the UK*. Fatherhood Institute, 2017; Parkes et al., *Growing up in Scotland: Father-child relationships and child socio-emotional wellbeing*. Scottish Government, 2017; Cano et al., A matter of time: Father involvement and child cognitive outcomes. *Journal of Marriage and Family, 81*(1), 164–184, 2019). Nevertheless, caregiving fathers have been observed to face numerous challenges as they attempt to take an active role in the caregiving of their children. This book identifies such challenges as 'fatherhood forfeits' and presents existing literature in this area alongside empirical data to explore the experiences and perceptions of caregiving fathers in the workplace.

© The Author(s), under exclusive license to Springer Nature Switzerland AG 2022
J. Kelland, *Caregiving Fathers in the Workplace*,
https://doi.org/10.1007/978-3-030-97971-3_1

This chapter outlines the drivers that prompted this research and its importance is explored. It then moves to discuss how the role of father is changing and it is suggested that despite this context of purported change, a climate of minimal actual change prevails. It concludes by outlining the structure of the book and the methods employed within the empirical data collection.

Keywords Fathers • Parents • Flexible Working • Breadwinner • Fatherhood forfeit • Discrimination

Why This Book? Why Now?

There are many reasons why a book that focuses on the perceptions and experiences of caregiving fathers at work is both pertinent and necessary. However, before embarking on this discussion it is appropriate to define the term 'caregiving father' within this context as it is integral to both the empirical research study and the wider examination of the issues within this book. A 'caregiving father' is identified as a father who is involved in the explicit care of their children such as changing nappies, playing, reading stories and indirect care such as purchasing the child's clothes (Cohen-Bendahan et al., 2015). This book focuses on caregiving fathers who combine caregiving and paid employment, navigating or attempting to navigate between these two spheres on a regular basis. The rationale for an exploration of the importance of exploring the experiences and perceptions of caregiving fathers at this time can be summarised into six central explanations.

Firstly, whilst existing research has previously observed that caregiving fathers experience negative peer relations and social mistreatment, there is a lack of detail and depth regarding the way in which this emerges in the context of UK workplaces. A fuller understanding of the challenges facing UK caregiving fathers in the workplace makes addressing them and their minimisation more likely; thus, an exploration of this nature will promote an improved workplace experience for this grouping.

Secondly, whilst it is widely acknowledged that fathers face barriers in obtaining working arrangements that enable caregiving, a wider understanding of the way in which this manifests is needed, specifically regarding at what point in the recruitment and selection process the barriers emerge. It is expected that such increased knowledge will result in improved effectiveness of organisational recruitment, selection and ultimately improved retention processes (Eriksson & Kristensen, 2014; Li et al., 2018; Moran & Koslowski, 2019). This is particularly pertinent with regard to the recruitment of millennials due to the alignment of such arrangements with notions of millennial expectations (Brant & Castro, 2019).

Thirdly, existing research has found that organisations can expect to have increased work performance from caregivers who feel supported in organisations and have reduced levels of work family conflict, highlighting a distinct business benefit of addressing the issues raised within this book (Plaisier et al., 2015; Kelliher et al., 2019).

Fourthly, the UK labour market can be seen to be in a current state of flux. The full implications of 'Brexit' are yet to emerge; however, recruitment challenges are starting to emerge in some industries (such as haulage) due to increased shortages in the labour market and therefore the need to maximise the talent and skills of the workforce is imperative (CIPD, 2021). Similarly, the full impact of the Covid-19 pandemic in the UK is yet to be established. It has been predicted by some (ACAS, 2021) that as a consequence of experiences during the pandemic there will be an increase in requests from fathers to access flexible working; therefore, wider understanding of the experiences of these individuals is specifically pertinent.

Fifthly, support for adherence to the full-time male breadwinner ideology which can be considered to "pull men out of the home and push women into it" implies that any revolution towards gender equality in the UK is further away than may appear on the surface (Berdahl & Moon, 2013: 343; Esping-Andersen et al., 2013). Through exploring the experiences and perceptions of caregiving fathers, this book will seek deeper understanding regarding the differential impact of parenthood on mothers and fathers, potentially uncovering explanations for disparities between parents and work. It is suggested in this book that a greater understanding of the obstacles faced by caregiving fathers in the workplace will facilitate an equal sharing of work and family commitments for both parents and thus enable a reduction in associated gendered economic inequalities such as the gender pay gap (Cooke & Fuller, 2018).

Finally, such an exploration is necessary due to the many benefits to children and parents of fathers having an active role in caregiving. Children within households which comprise a caregiving father have been found to have improved outcomes when compared to those that do not, specifically with regard to doing better at school, having higher self-esteem and being less likely to get into trouble as teenagers (Levtov et al., 2015; Burgess & Davies, 2017; Parkes et al., 2017; Cano et al., 2019). Similarly, having a highly involved father has been found to be associated with increased cognitive competence, empathy and reduced sex-stereotyped beliefs (Pruett, 1985; Radin, 1994; Pleck, 1997). This is supported by Jane van Zyl, Chief Executive Officer of UK work-life balance charity 'Working Families', who stated "the benefits of getting it right are huge – not just for the organisation and the individual, but for society as a whole". She continued "It's in every employers' interest to make sure their workplace culture and employee benefits support fathers to get a good work life balance, and allows them to play a meaningful role in their children's lives from the start" (van Zyl, 2021).

Before introducing the study itself and explaining the structure of the book it is necessary to set the context. To this end, the landscape for contemporary working parents will now be explored, outlining the current conceptualisations of modern fatherhood and exploring the opportunities and challenges inherent within these conceptualisations.

CONTEMPORARY WORKING PARENTS

The landscape for contemporary working parents is consistently suggested to have moved towards a position of increased equality in relation to both the work and home spheres. It is widely acknowledged that modern fathers undertake a more active role in the 'hands on' parenting of their children than in previous generations and that mothers are making an increasing contribution to the labour market (Gatrell et al., 2014). This change is in part substantiated by UK societal and economic statistics which show a significant increase in the participation of mothers in the workplace over time, with 73.2% of contemporary couple families comprising two working parents (Office for National Statistics, 2019).

Fatherhood in modern UK society is consistently purported to have shifted away from archetypal 1950s imagery in which a father has primary associations to the workplace. Conceptualisations of fathers as being both physically and emotionally distant from the family appear as an outdated representation of modern fatherhood (Burnett et al., 2013). Such traditional notions of parenting are suggested to have been replaced by "more egalitarian viewpoints", in which domestic responsibilities are shared by contemporary couples, with both parents undertaking employment outside of the home, regularly moving between family and employment (Budworth et al., 2008: 10; Norman, 2010; Connolly et al., 2016; Haas & Hwang, 2015). This points to an authentic move away from more traditional breadwinning ideologies, in which fathers are the "male dominant economic actor" (Connolly et al., 2016: 2), towards a model of greater involvement and equality in parenting. Such an increase in equality with regard to parental involvement has been widely acknowledged in reports undertaken by the Trade Union Congress (2017), Advisory, Conciliation and Arbitration Service (2017) and House of Commons Women and Equalities Select Committee (2017). In turn, the practices of working fathers appear to have evolved. Research by 'Working Families' found that the vast majority of fathers in their study stated that childcare would be a key consideration when making their career decisions and researchers observed that the majority of fathers in their study regularly dropped their children into childcare facilities, such as school or nursery before going to work (Modern Families Index, 2019).

The UK policy agenda is reflective of a move towards the greater involvement of fathers in caregiving through numerous legislative changes introduced, such as the stand-alone rights to paternity leave in 2003. More recently, April 2011 saw the introduction of shared parental leave (SPL) echoing societal moves toward an increasingly equal division of parenting responsibilities. At its inception, SPL was described as a step towards challenging the norms for working mothers, enabling a reduction in the barriers women face when trying to fill senior roles and at the same time permitting an increased involvement for fathers in parenting their children. Some have gone as far as to say that the main premise of SPL was the creation of a "gender-equal utopia" (The Guardian, 6th February, 2017). However, this purported aspiration seems to bear little resemblance to the reality for UK working parents with the take-up of SPL still 'exceptionally low', with around 2% of those eligible taking advantage of the leave (Howlett, 2020). Given that research has suggested that fathers often use annual leave after the birth of a child rather than paternity leave, perhaps this low level of take-up of SPL is unsurprising (Mercer, 2017). Potential explanations for low take-up of SPL have been proposed to be associated with lack of clarity, financial implications, emotional factors (such as maternal guilt and not wanting to give anything up) and social factors associated with gender role stereotypes (Banister & Kerrane, 2017; Hacohen et al., 2018). Such low uptake levels of SPL are indicative that the purported shifts in the level of involvement of fathers might not, in reality, have translated into the day-to-day working arrangements of fathers and this is observable within flexible working arrangements more widely.

A key indicator of an increased position of equality would be a wider uptake of working arrangements that allow for caregiving, such as flexible working which can be conceptualised as a central mechanism to assist with the management of the two spheres of work and family. However, the division of such working arrangements remains gendered, implying that a position of equality between parents remains an aspiration rather than a reality. For example, fathers have been found to be much more likely than mothers to believe they don't have access to flexible working arrangements, such as flexi-time, working part-time and working from home (O'Brien et al., 2018). Similarly, ACAS have proposed that fathers are less aware of the flexible working options available to them and suggested that whilst mothers are well informed about all of their options with regard to flexibility when they become mothers, the position for fathers is more opaque. The ACAS report noted that some fathers have been found to conceal any work-life conflict that they may encounter and report being afraid to ask for greater flexibility (Mercer, 2017).

Such findings build on the work of Scott and Clery (2013), who found little evidence for an increase in the sharing of roles, with 38% of their participants believing that the model of full-time father and part-time mother continues to be conceptualised as the most effective way to combine work and family life. More specifically, fathers are widely observed to continue to dominate the realms of full-time employment, adhering to more traditional conventions of breadwinning, rather than adopting part-time approaches (Gregory & Connolly, 2008; Speight et al., 2013). Many academics suggest that despite the increasing contribution of mothers in the labour market and a supposedly increasingly active role of fathers in the parenting their children, a climate of minimal actual change with regard to the working hours of fathers prevails (Shows & Gerstel, 2009; Aumann et al., 2011).

Research findings are indicative that mothers continue to undertake the larger share of caregiving; even when they earn more and work longer hours than their partners, they still carry the majority of parenting duties (Poole et al., 2013; Lyonette & Crompton, 2015). With mothers observed to consistently have more direct involvement with children, including positive engagement activities, indirect care and decision-making, than fathers, irrespective of their working hours or salary circumstances (Poole et al.,

2013). Similarly, data from the Office for National Statistics (ONS) tell us that whilst 3 in 10 mothers with a child aged 14 years and under said they have reduced their working hours for childcare reasons, only 1 in 20 fathers had. They continue that when both working parents in heterosexual couples are considered, a father is far more likely to be in full-time work, aligning to breadwinning mentalities. Whereas for mothers, they are more likely to be taking on the primary responsibility for the children in the family and undertaking less work outside the home in a way that facilitates this caregiving role, with 92.6% of fathers with dependent children working 30 or more hours a week compared with 75.1% of mothers (ONS, 2019). Therefore, whilst many academics confidently espouse a new type of fatherhood, it appears a climate of minimal actual change regarding paternal working patterns remains, and the ideology of male breadwinners and female homemakers remains (Haas & Hwang, 2015; Moran & Koslowski, 2019). Such ideologies can be considered to have potentially detrimental implications for both parents; specifically for women it is suggested that this can be associated with their fortunes at work continuing to fall significantly short of those enjoyed by men (Eikhof, 2012).

More recent findings by the ONS (2018) provides supporting evidence of a link between parenthood and the continuation of the gender pay gap, in which men's full-time average earnings are reported to be 9.1% higher than women. Such a prevailing gap in the UK is somewhat surprising as it exists in a climate in which more women graduate than men (UCAS, 2016). ONS data demonstrate that the gap does not appear to emerge to any significant extent until later in life. However, once employees are in their 40s, the gender pay gap starts to widen in increasing levels until retirement (ONS, 2018). It is widely acknowledged that the key difference between men and women during this period is the gendered impact of having children and the consequent implications of this on the working hours of parents (Elming et al., 2016; EHRC, 2016, Committee Evidence; Fawcett Society, 2018). The prevalence of the differential impact of parenthood on mothers and fathers is such that this issue was discussed by the House of Commons Women and Equalities Select Committee and highlighted as playing a part in the continuation of the pay gap (House of Commons Publications, 2016). This is supported by Rubery and Rafferty (2013) who propose that identifying men as the 'core' workforce (full-time) and women as the 'periphery' (part-time) workforce is key to the maintenance of the gender pay gap. This concept is evidenced through the statistics in this area, as despite potential changes in the landscape and an increasing number of men working part-time (Wang et al., 2013), women remain three times more likely to be in part-time employment than men (ONS, 2017). This supports existing research which has observed that whilst in principle the policy environment has shifted from assumptions of a male breadwinner to dual earners, due to severe constraints on mothers' labour market participation, women continue to earn half the lifetime earnings of men (Warren et al., 2009). It is possible that recent UK legislation which now requires employers with over 250 employees to publish gender pay gap data annually will encourage change in this area; however, it is too early to be able to provide evidence of this change (The Equality Act, 2010-Gender Pay Gap Reporting Regulations, 2017).

It appears that notwithstanding the many societal and legislative changes identified in this chapter the actual and expected working arrangements of parents appear to remain intertwined with notions of breadwinning and homemaking, implying that any revolution towards gender equality is further away than may appear on the surface (Esping-Andersen et al., 2013). This book resides within the context of this juxtaposition of an apparent societal discourse of a caregiving and involved father (Gatrell et al., 2014) within a climate of limited evidential change to contemporary working patterns.

THE 'FATHERHOOD FORFEIT STUDY'

This book blends empirical data academic literature and grey literature to illustrate the current state of play for caregiving fathers in the workplace, primarily focusing on the 'Fatherhood Forfeit Study'.

The 'Fatherhood Forfeit Study' explored the workplace experiences and perceptions of caregiving fathers in the UK through the lens of the actors involved in the process. Specifically, the study utilised working fathers, working mothers and managers as participants with the aim of obtaining a broader view of workplace experiences and perceptions than currently is believed to exist. Working fathers were chosen due to their ability to provide insight into their own personal experiences and this grouping comprised participants who could be classified as more traditional working fathers who worked full-time and align to notions of breadwinning, and caregiving fathers who were conceptualised as having caregiving responsibilities and thus align to more flexible working arrangements. In addition, working mothers and managers were identified as participants as they can provide a valuable insight into the workplace experiences of caregiving fathers. Such 'social actors', whose association with caregiving fathers varies from being married to a caregiving father, working alongside a caregiving father or managing a caregiving father, were believed to be essential in the exploration of this issue.

Quantitative and qualitative data are employed within the study with the aim of obtaining a fuller picture regarding the experiences and perceptions of caregiving fathers in the workplace. A key benefit of the mixed-methods approach is that it enables the triangulation of data (Creswell, 2009) which is considered to be a critical element of research in social sciences (Denzin & Lincoln, 2005), allowing the "most persuasive evidence" to be obtained (Freshwater, 2007: 141). Such a complementary method of exploring social phenomena is arguably the most effective way to explore the perceptions and experiences of caregiving fathers, providing broader perspectives, greater than mono method research designs would be able to (Bryman, 2008; Fielding, 2010; Azorín & Cameron, 2010). By utilising both quantitative and qualitative data it is envisaged that the benefits of both methods will be maximised and the respective weaknesses of each method will be avoided (Tashakkori & Teddlie, 2010). Despite the differing nature of the data, they can be considered compatible due to being viewed as different ends of a continuum rather than complete opposites (Newman et al., 1998).

Quantitative data were obtained through an online vignette survey with manager participants and such a vignette method is popular in gender- and family-related research (Karpinska et al., 2011) and was chosen as it permitted a wider exploration of human actions than a traditional questionnaire (Ganong & Coleman, 2006; Wallander, 2009). Vignettes involve investigating participant responses to a hypothetical scenario, requiring them to make a choice in response to a scenario which is proposed to have the benefit of resulting in more genuine responses (Ganong & Coleman, 2006). This is of particular importance when participants might be aware that their choices will be judged (Bryman & Bell, 2011). Parental decision-making regarding the extent of involvement in caregiving can be considered to be fraught with judgements and therefore this was deemed to be a highly suitable method.

The online vignette survey established at the start of the study if parental gender and caregiving responsibilities had any real-world implications with regard to workplace perceptions in the context of recruitment and selection. It involved participants rating four fictitious applicants: a father applicant for a part-time role, a mother applicant for a part-time role and a mother and father applicant for a full-time role. Specifically, the online vignette survey sought to explore if parental gender impacts upon how fictitious parent applicants are rated against the measures of 'perceived competence', 'hireability', 'promotability' and 'workplace competence'. Utilising the same vignette, focus groups with manager participants were employed to take a more qualitative stance, with the aim of identifying the rationale for the ratings received by the caregiving father, portrayed as a part-time applicant in the online vignette survey, and to permit a deeper understanding of the perceptions of caregiving fathers. The final method employed within the 'Fatherhood Forfeit Study' consisted of qualitative semi-structured interviews with managers and working parents to gain a greater understanding of the workplace experiences and perceptions of caregiving fathers. Through employing questions informed by the review of the literature and the outcomes of the focus groups and online vignette survey the semi-structured interviews created an opportunity to explore the experiences and perceptions of caregiving fathers from the viewpoint of the key social actors.

WHAT IS THE FATHERHOOD FORFEIT?

The study discussed within this book highlights the specific challenges faced by caregiving fathers when they attempt to take an active role in the parenting of their children which is identified as the 'fatherhood forfeit'. 'Fatherhood forfeits' have been found within both the quantitative and qualitative data presented. Initially, the quantitative data illustrate how fathers are less likely than mothers to obtain a job role that is conducive to taking an active role in caregiving (in this study, a part-time role); thus, they face a 'fatherhood forfeit'. The book continues to investigate the 'fatherhood forfeit' through exploration of qualitative data, extending the concept to encompass the attitudinal barriers faced by caregiving fathers, identifying that fathers forfeit a more positive workplace experience when seeking to adopt working practices that facilitate active involvement in the caregiving of their children. The nature of the forfeit within the qualitative data relates to caregiving fathers facing 'Where is Mum?' comments and judgements of 'Unconventionality', obtaining less workplace support than mothers for caregiving activities and social mistreatment (such as negative judgement and mockery). Thus, caregiving fathers are identified as encountering facing a set of forfeits that are twofold.

Fathers face a forfeit of being less likely to obtain a role conducive to taking an active role in caregiving and forfeit a positive workplace experience if they do obtain such a role (or in the attempt to obtain it.)

Throughout this book it is suggested that the 'fatherhood forfeit' in its different guises acts as a force that pushes caregiving fathers towards the maintenance of breadwinning norms in an attempt to either avoid them, or as a consequence of them. Additionally, it is suggested that the 'fatherhood forfeit' impacts upon the workplace experiences and perceptions of caregiving fathers creating a significant barrier to fathers in undertaking an active role in the caregiving of their children.

STRUCTURE OF THE BOOK

Existing research is explored in depth within this book, investigating the workplace implications for fathers in paid employment who have caregiving responsibilities for children, which are believed to be integral to notion of contemporary fatherhood. The work and family research arena is well established and largely consistent in espousing that whilst mothers face numerous challenges when combining work and family, knowledge regarding the experience of fathers is more disparate and often under researched within the literature (Fuegen et al., 2004; Correll et al., 2007; Burnett et al., 2013; Kelliher et al., 2019).

This book explores the workplace experience and perceptions of caregiving fathers through six chapters. The 'fatherhood forfeit' is offered as a potential explanation as to why so many fathers remain in the role of the family breadwinner, despite many desiring to take on additional responsibilities for the caregiving of their children, charting the existing academic literature alongside the specific research project presented here. The format of the remaining chapters is as follows:

Chapter 2: Caregiving Fathers and the 'Fatherhood Forfeit'

This chapter sets the context of the study and explores how the fatherhood forfeit emerged within the quantitative data. This involves exploring key literature alongside recent reports and data from ONS, Working Families and House of Commons Select Committees. It outlines the historical, legislative and political landscape for caregiving fathers in the UK, and the way in which these have impacted on both labour market participation and the division of parental responsibilities. It then presents quantitative survey data obtained through the online vignette survey part of the 'Fatherhood Forfeit Study' which is suggestive that fathers face a 'fatherhood forfeit' when they apply for part-time work to enable an active involvement in the caregiving of their children.

Chapter 3: Parental Gender Stereotyping and 'Think Child–Think Mum'

This chapter explores the way in which existing literature offers explanations as to why mothers are often considered to be the primary parent. It includes discussion of gendered stereotypes, their influence on the norms of behaviour and the existence of gendered behavioural expectations within the workplace for parents. It continues by presenting the qualitative data obtained through semi-structured interviews and focus groups within the 'Fatherhood Forfeit Study' to demonstrate how participants reported an assumption that the mother is always the primary parent and the father was placed in a secondary role regardless of the working arrangements of the parents. The chapter outlines how any deviation from this more traditional pattern was conceptualised as unconventional. Throughout the chapter, data are linked to the existing academic terrain outlining the ways in which this work both corresponds with and contradicts existing knowledge.

Chapter 4: 'Fathers Obtain Less Workplace Support Than Mothers for Caregiving'

This chapter explores both key literature and recent reports to investigate workplace outcomes when fathers challenge the purported social norms by seeking more flexible working patterns to enable an active role in the caregiving of their children. As with previous chapters, the qualitative data obtained in the 'Fatherhood Forfeit Study' through semi-structured interviews and focus groups are presented to illustrate ways in which fathers obtain less workplace support than mothers for caregiving. It is further proposed that workplace support for fathers to undertake caregiving is often conditional and context specific. Synergies are consistently made between existing academic knowledge and findings from the 'Fatherhood Forfeit Study'.

Chapter 5: 'Social Mistreatment of Caregiving Fathers'

This chapter presents existing knowledge regarding social and workplace outcomes when fathers challenge the purported social norms by taking an active role in the caregiving of their children and adopting, or seeking to adopt more flexible working patterns. It has specific focus on the nature and impact of sanctions for caregiving fathers. The chapter explores the qualitative data obtained from semi-structured interviews and focus groups within the 'Fatherhood Forfeit Study' utilising illustrative quotes to demonstrate the social mistreatment of caregiving fathers. It focuses in detail on the most widely recurring themes of negative judgement' 'suspicion, mockery', struggling with friendships and being viewed as idle'. It highlights the ways in which this work aligns with existing research.

Chapter 6: What Is Next for Caregiving Fathers?

The final chapter comprises a practical outline of key learnings from the 'Fatherhood Forfeit Study' and existing research on ways that organisations and caregiving fathers themselves can attempt to avoid the 'fatherhood forfeits' as presented in this book and improve working life for parents. Throughout this chapter, reference is made to the implications of the Covid-19 pandemic for working parents and examples of contemporary organisational best practice are charted.

CHAPTER SUMMARY

This chapter has introduced the structure of the book and outlined the key drivers for its publication. It has been highlighted that an exploration into the experiences and perceptions of caregiving fathers has the potential to reduce inequality within the workplace for both mothers and fathers. Such inequalities are highlighted as being of increasing importance in contemporary workplaces, with factors such as the gender pay gap and the impact of Covid-19 lockdowns increasing interest in exploring the gendered nature of workplace treatment of parents.

'The Fatherhood Forfeit Study' has been briefly introduced within this chapter, to underpin a more in-depth exploration in Chap. 2.

References

ACAS. (2021, June). *Employer expectations of working practices after Coronavirus, Great Britain*. Available at: https://www.acas.org.uk/employer-poll-working-practices-after-covid-19-june-2021/html. Accessed 8 Nov 2021.

Advisory, Conciliation and Arbitration Service (ACAS). (2017). Flexible working for parents returning to work: Maintaining career development. http://www.acas.org.uk/media/pdf/k/7/Flexible-working-for-parents-returning-to-work-maintaining-career-development.pdf

Aumann, K., Galinsky, E., & Matos, K. (2011). *The new male mystique*. Families and Work Institute.

Azorín, J. M., & Cameron, R. (2010). The application of mixed methods in organisational research: A literature review. *Electronic Journal of Business Research Methods, 8*(2), 95–105.

Banister, E., & Kerrane, B. (2017). Can men mother? Employed men's experiences of shared parental leave and conceptions of fatherhood. In *13th conference on gender, marketing and consumer behaviour*.

Berdahl, J. L., & Moon, S. H. (2013). Workplace mistreatment of middle class workers based on sex, parenthood and caregiving. *Journal of Social Issues, 69*(2), 341–366. https://doi.org/10.1111/josi.12018

Brant, K. K., & Castro, S. L. (2019). You can't ignore millennials: Needed changes and a new way forward in entitlement research. *Human Resource Management Journal, 29*(4), 527–538.

Bryman, A. (2008). *Social research methods* (3rd ed.). Oxford University Press.

Bryman, A., & Bell, E. (2011). *Business research methods* (3rd ed.). Oxford University Press.

Budworth, M., Enns, J., & Rowbotham, K. (2008). Shared identity and strategic choice in dual career couples. *Gender in Management: An International Journal, 23*(2), 103–119. https://doi.org/10.1108/17542410810858312

Burgess, A., & Davies, J. (2017). *Cash or carry? Fathers combining work and care in the UK*. Fatherhood Institute. Available at: http://www.fatherhoodinstitute.org/wp-content/uploads/2017/12/Cash-and-carry-Full-Report-PDF.pdf. Accessed 28 Sept 2020.

Burnett, S. B., Gatrell, C. J., Cooper, C. L., & Sparrow, P. (2013). Fathers at work: A ghost in the organizational machine. *Gender, Work and Organization, 20*(6), 632–646. https://doi.org/10.1111/gwao.12000

Cano, T., Perales, F., & Baxter, J. (2019). A matter of time:father involvement and child cognitive outcomes. *Journal of Marriage and Family, 81*(1), 164–184.

CIPD. (2021). *Addressing skills and labour shortages Post Brexit*. Available at: https://www.cipd.co.uk/Images/addressing-skills-labour-shortages-post-brexit_tcm18-102313.pdf. Accessed 8 Nov 2021.

Cohen-Bendahan, C. C., Beijers, R., van Doornen, L. J., & de Weerth, C. (2015). Explicit and implicit caregiving interests in expectant fathers; do endogenous and exogenous oxytocin and vasopressin matter? *Infant Behavior & Development, 41*(November), 26–37.

Connolly, S., Aldrich, M., O'Brien, M., Speight, S., & Poole, E. (2016). Britain's slow movement to a gender egalitarian equilibrium: Parents and employment in the UK 2001–13. *Work, Employment and Society, 30*(5), 838–857.

Cooke, L. P., & Fuller, S. (2018). Class differences in establishment pathways to fatherhood wage premiums. *Journal of Marriage and Family, 80*(3), 737–751.

Correll, S., Benard, S., & Paik, I. (2007). Getting a job: Is there a motherhood penalty? *American Journal of Sociology, 112*(5), 1297–1338.

Creswell, J. (2009). *Research design: Qualitative, quantitative and mixed method approaches* (3rd ed.). Sage.

Denzin, N. K., & Lincoln, Y. S. (2005). *The Sage handbook of qualitative research.* Sage.

EHRC. (2016). *Response to call for written evidence from the Equality and Human Rights Commission.* Available at: http://data.parliament.uk/WrittenEvidence/ CommitteeEvidence.svc/EvidenceDocument/Women%20and%20Equalities/ Gender%20Pay%20Gap/written/25494.html. Accessed 8 Nov 2021.

Eikhof, D. (2012). A double edged sword; twenty first century workplace trends and gender equality. *Gender in Management: An International Journal, 27*(1), 7–22.

Elming, W., Joyce, R., Dias, M. C., & Institute of Fiscal Studies. (2016, August). *The gender wage gap.* Available at: https://www.ifs.org.uk/publications/8428. Accessed 28 Sept 2018.

Eriksson., & Kristensen (2014). Eriksson, T. and Kristensen, N., 2014. Wages or fringes? Some evidence on trade-offs and sorting. *Journal of Labor Economics, 32*(4), pp. 899–928.

Esping-Andersen, G., Boertien, D., Bonke, J., & Gracia, P. (2013). Couple specialisation in multiple equilibria. *European Sociological Review, 29*(6), 1280–1294.

Fawcett Society. (2018). *Close the gender pay gap.* Available at: https://www.faw-cettsociety.org.uk/close-gender-pay-gap. Accessed 28 Sept 2018.

Fielding, N. (2010). Mixed methods in the real world. *International Journal of Social Research Methodology, 13*(2), 127–138. https://doi.org/10.1080/ 13645570902996186

Freshwater, D. (2007). Reading mixed methods research; contexts for criticism. *Journal of Mixed Methods Research, 1*, 134. https://doi.org/10.1177/ 1558689806298578

Fuegen, K., Biernat, M., Haines, E., & Deaux, K. (2004). Mothers and fathers in the workplace: How gender and parental status influence judgments of job-related competence. *Journal of Social Issues, 60*(4), 737–754.

Ganong, L. H., & Coleman, M. (2006). Multiple segment factorial vignette designs. *Journal of Marriage and Family, 68*(2), 455–468.

Gatrell, C. J., Burnett, S. B., Cooper, C. L., & Sparrow, P. (2014). Parents, perceptions and belonging: Exploring flexible working among UK fathers and mothers. *British Journal of Management, 25*(3), 473–487.

Gregory, M., & Connolly, S. (2008). Feature: The price of reconciliation: Part-time work, families and women's satisfaction. *The Economic Journal, 118*(February), 1–7.

Haas, L., & Hwang, C. P. (2015). It's about time!: Company support for fathers' entitlement to reduced work hours in Sweden. *Social Politics: International Studies in Gender, State & Society, 23*(1), 142–167. https://doi.org/10.1093/sp/jxv033

Hacohen, R., Likki, T., Londakova, K., Rossiter, J., & Government Equalities Office. (2018). *Return to work- parental decision making.* Available at: https://assets.publishing.service.gov.uk/government/uploads/system/uploads/attachment_data/file/705898/Return_to_work-parental_decision_making.pdf. Accessed 15 Apr 2019.

House of Commons Publications. (2016). *The gender pay gap-second report of session.* Available at: https://publications.parliament.uk/pa/cm201516/cmselect/cmwomeq/584/584.pdf. Accessed 8 Nov 2021.

House of Commons Women and Equalities Select Committee. (2017). *Fathers in the workplace inquiry.* Available at: https://www.parliament.uk/business/committees/committees-a-z/commons-select/women-and-equalities-committee/inquiries/parliament-2015/fathers-and-the-workplace-16-17/. Accessed 4 Apr 2019.

Howlett, E. (2020, September 7). Shared parent leave uptake still 'exceptional low' research finds. *People Management Magazine.* https://www.peoplemanagement.co.uk/news/articles/shared-parental-leave-uptake-still-exceptionally-low#gref

Karpinska, K., Henkens, K., & Schippers, J. (2011). The recruitment of early retirees: A vignette study of the factors that affect managers' decisions. *Ageing and Society, 31*(4), 570–589. https://doi.org/10.1017/S0144686X10001078

Kelliher, C., Richardson, J., & Boiarintseva, G. (2019). All of work? All of life? Reconceptualising work-life balance for the 21st century. *Human Resource Management Journal, 29*(2), 97–112.

Levtov, R., Van Der Gaag, N., Greene, M., Kaufman, M., & Barker, G. (2015). *State of the world's fathers: A MenCare advocacy publication.* Promundo, Rutgers, Save the Children, Sonke Gender Justice, and the MenEngage Alliance. Available at: https://www.savethechildren.net/sites/default/files/libraries/state-of-the-worlds-fathers_12-june-2015.pdf. Accessed 28 Sept 2018.

Li, A., Butler, A., & Bagger, J. (2018). Depletion or expansion? Understanding the effects of support policy use on employee work and family outcomes. *Human Resource Management Journal, 28*(2), 216–234.

Lyonette, C., & Crompton, R. (2015). Sharing the load? Partners' relative earnings and the division of domestic labour. *Work, Employment and Society, 29*(1), 23–40.

Mercer, M. (2017). *Flexible working for parents returning to work: Maintaining career development.* ACAS. Available at: https://www.employment-studies.co.uk/resource/flexible-working-parents-returning-work. Accessed 8 Nov 2021

Moran, J., & Koslowski, A. (2019). Making use of work-family balance entitlements: How to support fathers with combining employment and caregiving. *Community Work Family, 22,* 111–128.

Newman, I., Benz, C. R., & Ridenour, C. S. (1998). *Qualitative-quantitative research methodology: Exploring the interactive continuum.* SIU Press.

Norman, H. (2010). *Involved fatherhood: An analysis of the conditions associated with paternal involvement in childcare and housework.* Unpublished doctoral thesis, University of Manchester. Available at: https://www.escholar.manchester.ac.uk/uk-ac-man-scw:163780

O'Brien, M., Aldrich, M., Connolly, S., Cook, R., & Speight, S. (2018). *Inequalities in access to paid maternity and paternity leave and flexible work: Report.*

Office for National Statistics (2017). *Families in the labour market.* Available at: https://www.ons.gov.uk/peoplepopulationandcommunity/birthsdeathsandmarriages/families/bulletins/familiesandhouseholds/2017

Office of National Statistics (2018). *Understanding the gender pay gap in the UK.* Available at: https://www.ons.gov.uk/employmentandlabourmarket/peopleinwork/earningsandwor kinghours/articles/understandingthegender paygapintheuk/2018-01-17

Office for National Statistics. (2019). *Families in the labour market.* Available at: https://www.ons.gov.uk/employmentandlabourmarket/peopleinwork/employmentandemployeetypes/articles/familiesandthelabourmarketengland/2019. Accessed 6 Nov 2021.

Parkes, A., Riddell, J., Wight, D., & Buston, K. (2017). *Growing up in Scotland: Father-child relationships and child socio-emotional wellbeing.* Scottish Government.

Plaisier, I., Broese van Groenou, M. I., & Keuzenkamp, S. (2015). Combining work and informal care: The importance of caring organisations. *Human Resource Management Journal, 25*(2), 267–280.

Pleck, J. (1997). Paternal Involvement: Levels, sources and consequences. In M. E. Lamb (Ed.), *The role of the father in child development* (pp. 66–103), 3rd edn. New York: Wiley.

Poole, E., Speight, S., O'Brien, M., Connolly, S., & Aldrich, M. (2013). *Fathers involvement with children and couple relationships* (ESRC Briefing paper). Available at: http://www.modernfatherhood.org/wp-content/uploads/2014/10/Fathers-relationships-briefing-paper.pdf. Accessed 1 Oct 2018.

Pruett, K. D. (1985). Children of the father mothers: Infants of primary nurturing fathers. In J. D. Call, E. Galenson, & R. L. Tyson (Eds.), *Frontiers of infant psychiatry* (pp. 375–380). New York: Basic Books, Inc., 2.

Radin, N. (1994). 'Primary caregiving fathers in intact families', in A.E. Gottfried, & A.W. Gottfried (Eds.), *Redefining families: Implications for children's development* (pp.11–54). New York: Plenum.

Rubery, J., & Rafferty, A. (2013). Gender, recession and austerity in the UK. In M. Karamessini & J. Rubery (Eds.), *Women and austerity: The economic crisis and the future of gender equality*. Routledge, Part II, 7.

Scott, J., & Clery, E. (2013). *Gender roles: An incomplete revolution?* British Social Attitudes Survey, 30th Report. NatCen Social Research. Available at: http://www.bsa.natcen.ac.uk/media/38723/bsa30_full_report_final.pdf. Accessed 29 Oct 2018.

Shows, C., & Gerstel, N. (2009). Fathering, class, and gender: A comparison of physicians and emergency medical technicians. *Gender & Society, 23*(2), 161–187. https://doi.org/10.1177/0891243209333872

Speight, S., Poole, E., O'Brien, M., Connolly, S., & Aldrich, M. (2013). *Men and fatherhood: Who are today's fathers?* (ESRC Briefing paper). Available at: http://www.modernfatherhood.org/wp-content/uploads/2013/06/Who-are-todays-fathers-with-tables.pdf. Accessed 1 Oct 2018.

Tashakkori, A., & Teddlie, C. (2010). Putting the human back in "human research methodology": The researcher in mixed methods research. *Journal of Mixed Methods Research, 4*(4), 271–277.

The Equality Act, 2010-Gender Pay Gap Reporting Regulations. (2017). Available at: https://www.legislation.gov.uk/ukdsi/2017/9780111152010. Accessed 8 Nov 2021.

The Guardian, 6th February. (2017). *Utopian thinking; how to build a truly feminist society.* https://www.theguardian.com/commentisfree/2017/feb/06/utopian-thinking-build-truly-feminist-society

Trades Union Congress (TUC). (2017). *Better jobs for mums and dads.* Available at: https://www.tuc.org.uk/research-analysis/reports/better-jobs-mums-and-dads. Accessed 8 Nov 2021.

UCAS. (2016). *UCAS data reveals the numbers of men and women placed in over 150 higher education subjects.* UCAS Press. Available at: https://www.ucas.com/corporate/news-and-key-documents/news/ucas-data-reveals-numbers-men-and-women-placed-over-150-higher. Accessed 28 Sept 2018.

van Zyl, J. (2021). via email with Jasmine Kelland, 2nd August Advisory

Wang, W., Parker, K., & Taylor, P. (2013). *Breadwinner moms: Mothers are the sole or primary provider in four-in-ten households with children; public conflicted about the growing trend.* Pew Research Centre. Available at: http://www.pewsocialtrends.org/2013/05/29/breadwinner-moms/. Accessed 28 Sept 2018

Warren, T., Fox, E., & Pascall, G. (2009). Innovative social policies; implications for work-life balance amongst low-wages women in England. *Gender, Work and Organisation, 16*(1), 126–150. https://doi.org/10.1111/j. 1468-0432.2008.00433.x

Working Families. (2019). *Modern families' index.* Available at: https://www. workingfamilies.org.uk/wp-content/uploads/2019/02/BH_MFI_ Summary_Report_2019_Final.pdf. Accessed 4 Apr 2019.

Wallander (2009). 25 years of factorial surveys in sociology: A review. *Social Science Research, 38*(3), pp. 505–520.

CHAPTER 2

Caregiving Fathers and the 'Fatherhood Forfeit'

Abstract This chapter sets the context for the 'Fatherhood Forfeit Study' by charting the ways in which the historical, legislative and political landscape for caregiving fathers in the UK has altered over time. This is achieved through exploration of key literature, research reports and labour market data. Such an exploration highlights how societal changes have impacted upon both the labour market participation of both mothers and fathers and the subsequent division of parental responsibilities.

The chapter then moves to present data from the online vignette survey element of the 'Fatherhood Forfeit Study' which found that fathers are less likely than mothers to obtain part-time work to enable an active involvement in the caregiving of their children, and it introduces the notion of the 'fatherhood forfeit'.

Keywords Fathers • Discrimination • Breadwinner/Breadwinning • Labour Market • Legislation • Parents

HISTORICAL EVOLUTION OF WORK, SOCIETY AND PARENTHOOD

Academic literature is largely consistent in demonstrating that the nature of work, society and parenthood has altered over the last 150 years (Pleck & Pleck, 1997; Barnett & Hyde, 2001; Burnett et al., 2010). This chapter

J. Kelland, *Caregiving Fathers in the Workplace*, https://doi.org/10.1007/978-3-030-97971-3_2

explores these changes through initially exploring how the role of father has been conceptualised over time, placing the 'Fatherhood Forfeit Study' in context to permit a fuller understanding regarding the prevailing nature of traditional norms in the organisation of work and family life.

Early conceptualisations of fatherhood from the late eighteenth and early nineteenth centuries are indicative that family life was characterised by patriarchy, in which the role of father was considered by many to be that of 'moral overseer', 'protector' and 'educator', holding the ultimate responsibility and power within the family (Pleck & Pleck, 1997; Broughton & Rogers, 2007). Towards the mid to late nineteenth century this was observed to begin to alter due to the emergence of industrialisation which, for many, resulted in fathers undertaking an increased amount of paid work away from the family, thus becoming more separated and taking on the role of 'distant breadwinner' (Hilbrecht et al., 2008; Burnett et al., 2010). It is suggested that such absence resulted in increased decision-making authority of the mother within the home, diminishing the emphasis placed on the importance of father-child relationships and notions of ultimate responsibility and power resting with fathers (Cabrera et al., 2000; Burnett et al., 2010). At this time, it appears that the notion of a 'good father' began to be principally associated with the workplace, with responsibility for economic support and breadwinning replacing previous emphasis on 'moral leadership' (Allard et al., 2011; Crompton, 2002; Halford, 2006; Pleck & Pleck, 1997). It has been suggested that in turn, the role of mothers altered and mother began to take on primary responsibility for the domestic sphere and homemaking (Crompton, 2002; Allard et al., 2011).

After the turn of the century, the construction of the labour market began to alter, and by 1913 nearly a quarter of women worked outside of the home (Light, 1999). This was further compounded by the impact of World War I (1914–1918) which increased female labour market participation due to the absence of men who were away fighting in the war. After the war ended, female participation reduced again; however, it was to increase with the Great Depression of the late 1920s and early 1930s due to the unemployment of men and, for some, the impact of this was the start of a dilution of the role of the father as a provider (Elder, 1998; Bland, 2005). World War II (1939–1945) saw a further dramatic increase in female workforce participation due to an increased demand for workers, in which women (married and unmarried) undertook jobs that had been previously performed by men (Carr-Ruffino, 1993; Barnett & Hyde,

2001; Maund, 2001). Once again, this reduced after the war ended, with the 1950s being typified as an era in which the female homemaker and male provider was the prevailing cultural norm. However, the number of women in the labour market continued to increase from this point (Matthews & Rodin, 1989; Barnett & Hyde, 2001; National Child Development Survey, 2008). Alongside this, whilst the idealisation of fathers as 'distant breadwinners' remained dominant, a shift began to be observable towards a more 'modern-involved dad', with fathers once again having a key role in raising their children (Pleck, 1997; Cabrera et al., 2000: 127; Burnett et al., 2010). This change in the role of fathers, encouraged by post-war welfare policy, can be observed to steadily increase from this period (Smith, 1995; Perrons, 2009).

The composition of the labour market and the resultant repercussions on the division of household labour can be observed to shift again during the 1950s to the late 1970s due to changes with regard to birth control, such as the Abortion Act, 1967, the introduction of the contraceptive pill, and legislation such as the Equal Pay Act in 1970 and Sex Discrimination Act (1975). Similarly, during this time the labour market was shifting from being dominated by manufacturing industries such as coal and steel, towards service work, skilled non-manual work and 'knowledge work', a shift which removed issues such as physical strength that historically put men in a position of advantage in the workplace (Stanworth, 2000; Eikhof, 2012; Stuart et al., 2013). Additionally, such work offered greater flexibility in working hours, contracts and locations which eased the ability to combine a family and paid work and is likely to have contributed to the upward trend in the proportion of women in employment from the 1970s (Perrons, 2009; ONS, 2013). It has been proposed that during this time, many fathers were in 'crisis' due to the decline of the prevalence of the concept of the sole male breadwinner (Gillis, 2000; Brannen & Nilsen, 2006).

The social norm of the breadwinning father began to be diluted in the 1980s recession in which there was a sharp increase in inactivity rates, especially for men which saw the rise of dual earning families and female breadwinners which had implications on the division of caregiving responsibilities in the home (Besen, 2007; ONS, 2011). The further recession of the 1990s also saw a similar pattern with male economic inactivity rates being higher than those of women, and men being more likely to be made redundant than women (Department for Business, Innovation and Skills, 2013; ONS, 2011).

Along the way, numerous legislative changes have also had an impact on the division of parental responsibilities, most recently the Children and Families Act (2014) which gave employees the right to request flexible working (dependent on service) and the introduction of shared parental leave (SPL) in 2015. SPL permits working parents to share statutory leave after the birth of a child, subsequently allowing parents to choose how to allocate leave between them, making it easier for both parents to combine caregiving and labour market participation. Developments in legislative rights for fathers, such as SPL, can be considered a critical factor in facilitating the increase in female labour market participation and greater involvement of fathers in the caregiving of their children (National Child Development Survey, 2008; Eikhof, 2012).

As chronicled earlier in this chapter, many explanations have been offered to understand the evolution of the role of the modern-day father, with women's increasing labour market contribution, legislation and changes in structural composition of industries and families all having their part to play in the decline of the predominant breadwinning father model (Probert, 2005; Solomon, 2014). It is argued that,

> Traditional ideas have given way to more egalitarian viewpoints which deem it appropriate for both men and women to pursue paid employment outside of the home and also share responsibilities within the home. (Budworth et al., 2008: 104)

Similarly, the majority of parents have been reported as no longer believing that childcare is a main responsibility of mothers and that fathers have the main responsibility for providing for the family (EHRC, 2009). This is supported by ONS data which observed that the UK saw the highest rates of stay-at-home fathers since records began in 2012 (ONS, 2013), whilst 75.1% of mothers with dependent children worked outside of the home, pointing to a change in the division of labour both in the home and in the workplace (ONS, 2019).

The contemporary role of the father is argued to be more flexible than their historical counterparts, with modern fathers expected to mediate effectively between family and employment using flexible working practices (Burnett et al., 2013). Judgements aligned with being a good provider have been suggested to be no longer sufficient to affirm status as a 'good father' and that involvement in the care of children and a more active style of parenting is considered to be as, if not more, important

(Dermott, 2008; Lamb, 2008; Norman, 2010; Podnieks, 2016). The model of an 'involved father', who is an active 'hands-on' sharer of child caring responsibilities, engaged with family life, attentive and emotionally close to their children is observed to be increasing in both prevalence and importance (O'Brien, 2005; Solomon, 2014).

It is pertinent to note that whilst much research confidently espouses the existence of a new type of fatherhood, a significant gap between rhetoric and reality appears to remain for many contemporary parents. The model of 'modern male breadwinning', in which both parents work, but the mother works in a part-time capacity whilst the father works full-time, remains the dominant way in which families organise their domestic life (Berghammer, 2014; ONS, 2019). Whilst fathers might have greater involvement in parenting than in previous generations, it has been observed that fathers continue to spend less time caring for children than their spouses and the uptake of working arrangements to support caregiving by fathers, such as SPL, remains low (Aumann et al., 2011: 343; Shows & Gerstel, 2009; Wang et al., 2013; Powell, 2021). Such knowledge is indicative that breadwinning continues to be intrinsically associated with conceptualisations of the components of being a good father despite assertions of a changed ideology surrounding fatherhood (Townsend, 2002; Bergman & Hobson, 2002; Pocock, 2005; Holter, 2007; Wells & Sarkadi, 2012).

The prevailing dominance of the breadwinner father model seems at odds with the egalitarian approach widely accepted to be the cultural norm for contemporary parents, and therefore a wider exploration of the workplace perceptions and experiences of caregiving fathers is necessary to fully understand why parental gender disparity continues. Through the 'Fatherhood Forfeit Study' this book explores potential signals as to why the breadwinning model continues to dominate despite significant societal changes that are contrary to it, and 'fatherhood forfeits' are offered as a potential explanation for this phenomenon. To enable this discussion this chapter will now move to present data from the quantitative element of the 'Fatherhood Forfeit Study' which comprised an online vignette survey.

Fatherhood Forfeit Study: Online Vignette Survey

The design of the 'Fatherhood Forfeit Study' involved an online questionnaire based on a vignette created by the researcher, focus groups based on the same vignette and then semi-structured interviews which explored issues that emerged from the previous methods. An online vignette investigated how fictitious parents were rated by manager participants when applying for work and was employed as the first research method as it was considered to be appropriate to establish at the outset of the study if any differences existed between the ways in which working parents are perceived in contemporary workplaces. Previous research in a US context with student participants (Correll et al., 2007; Berdahl & Moon, 2013) adopted this approach and found gendered differentials. It was considered relevant to ascertain if the effect observed in the US with student participants emerged in a UK context with managers and working parents before embarking on a more in-depth exploration of the perceptions and experiences of caregiving fathers through qualitative analysis. This method also had the additional benefits of being quick to administer, cost-effective, able to reach large audiences and provides little room for bias (Whittaker, 2009; Collis & Hussey, 2013).

Whilst the online vignette captures essentially quantitative data, largely associated with a more positivistic paradigm of enquiry, overall, this study adopts a more qualitative approach which allows for deeper storytelling than a statistical model alone can possibly capture; thus, the philosophical approach of constructivism is adopted (Graham, 2011). Burke and Onwuegbuzie (2004: 19) propose that this approach of supporting qualitative research with a "closed-ended instrument to systematically measure certain factors" which emerged from the literature can benefit both types of data. It improves generalisability, expands knowledge and increases confidence in the conclusions drawn.

It was decided to administer the online vignette via the online platform of Qualtrics Software®, to remove additional information and protect anonymity (Maylor & Blackmon, 2005; Saunders et al., 2007). Qualtrics software was chosen due to its capacity to produce complex research tools, publish them via a web link and collect the results swiftly, with minimal cost implications (Barnhoorn et al., 2015). However, it is acknowledged that there are some limitations with this method, which include issues surrounding how long participants are prepared to spend completing an online task and participants being reluctant to write large amounts of self-completion responses. Concerns around response rates can also be an issue with online research methods because there is an inability to allow for probing or clarifying responses by the researchers (Sarantakos, 2005). As the online vignette was not being utilised alone and would be part of a mixed methods approach, the inability of an online approach to probe and clarify and possibly a low response rate was not considered to be a cause of significant concern as the focus groups and interview elements would probe more deeply into participant meanings and understandings. However, the issue of time spent to complete tasks was considered to be critical. To minimise the impact of this, the online vignette was kept focused and brief, particularly as participants were managers or busy parents and were voluntarily taking part in the research for no reward or gain.

The vignette method is popular in gender and family related research (Karpinska et al., 2011) and permits a wider exploration of human actions than a traditional questionnaire (Ganong & Coleman, 2006; Wallander, 2009). Vignettes involve investigating participant responses to a hypothetical scenario, requiring them to make a choice in response to the scenario which is proposed to have the benefit of resulting in more genuine responses (Ganong & Coleman, 2006). This is of particular importance when participants might be aware that their choices will be judged (Bryman & Bell, 2011). Parental decision-making regarding the extent of involvement caregiving can be considered to be fraught with judgements and therefore this was deemed as a highly suitable method.

The online vignette task included a briefing note, a role description for the fictitious vacancy and four summary CVs (see below). The summary CVs included applicants' career goals, parental status, educational history and past work experience, with all applicants being presented as highly productive (based on the format adopted by Cuddy et al., 2004, and Correll et al., 2007). Critical to the success of the vignette approach is that the scenario is convincing and this is a challenge with this approach (Miles & Huberman, 1994). To this end considerable attention was paid to the development of the vignettes to maximise their credibility and equality. To ensure this cognitive testing (Fevre et al., 2010; Lewis et al., 2013) was undertaken with post-graduate human resource management students which involved trialling the vignettes on three occasions. Consequently, adjustments were made based on feedback to minimise any areas of potential participant confusion which could be enhanced with greater clarity and also so that, as far as possible, the hypothetical applicants were considered to be equally well qualified for the role (as reported by Fuegen et al., 2004). The number of vignettes was purposefully small to minimise the participants' difficulties in processing the information, as if there is too much information to process, it can affect a participant's ability to visualise the hypothetical scenario (Rossi & Anderson, 1982; Karpinska et al., 2011).

As outlined above, care was spent in the description of a caregiving father and it was considered critical to the success of this study that a caregiving father was accurately represented in the vignettes. To this end, the

caregiving father and mother for the purposes of comparison were introduced in the vignette study as applying for a part-time (17.5 hours per
week) role by way of indicating, without being explicit, their caregiving
status. Caregiving status was reinforced with the following statements.

> He is applying for the part-time role as he wants to improve his work-life
> balance and spend more time with his children, twin boys aged two. (part-
> time father applicant)

> She is applying for this part-time job as she wants to improve her work-life
> balance as it will enable her to spend more time with her two children: Annie
> and Bobby, aged 18 months and three.

The initial sample was obtained through emailing a link to the Qualtrics
online vignette to managers and HR managers and they were asked to cir-
culate to managers within their organisation. This snowballing technique
was employed as it was considered to be suitable for participants who are
challenging to reach, such as managers (Karpinska et al., 2011). The initial
trawl of potential participants did not have as high a response rate as antici-
pated (Collis and Hussey, 2013) and therefore the researcher undertook a
second trawl which involved sending reminders to the previous potential
participants and sharing the Qualtrics ® link via the researcher's LinkedIn®
page, which resulted in a additional participants. LinkedIn was chosen as a
method of obtaining participants due to this platform being widely associated with managers and professionals (Skeels & Grudin, 2009). The sample was completed through posting a reminder via LinkedIn.

Once participants followed the Qualtrics web link, they were requested
to complete the consent form and state their gender; to protect anonymity
personal details such as age and ethnicity were not sought (in line, with
Gatrell et al., 2014).

In the next stage the participants were given a brief description of the
task, which was to rate applicants for a Customer Services Manager role at
a hypothetical bank entitled 'High Street Bank' and a role description.
This role was chosen as it was believed to be relatively gender-neutral, and
the researcher was keen to avoid professions such as nursing and engineers
in which there is a predominance of one gender over another (Howe,
2011). The task was in two parts (see below): part one required participants to read two applicant summary CVs (vignettes) for a part-time role,
Sienna and Max, and then rate those applicants. For part two, participants
were informed that the previous post holder had left employment and

participants were required to recruit for a full-time Customer Services Manager and needed to rate another two applicant summary CVs: Amelia and Oliver. The rating scores were 0–10 (10 being the highest, 0 being the lowest) based on the criteria of 'workplace commitment', 'hireability', 'promotability' and 'perceived competence'. These criteria and rating scale were devised by Correll et al. (2007) and adopted as they were considered to be well established in this area of research.

You are recruiting for a Part-Time (17.5 hours per week) Customer Services Manager. Please read these two summaries of job applicants. You will then be required to rate the suitability of each applicant for the Part-Time Customer Services Manager role and then rate the applicant.

Sienna Smith:

Sienna has five years' experience of being a Customer Services Manager at Village Bank in Lowshire. Prior to that she worked as a banking clerk. She is applying for this part-time job as she wants to improve her work life balance as it will enable her to spend more time with her two children; Annie and Bobby, aged 18 months and three. Her last appraisal ratings were excellent, and she achieved five staff nominations for Manager of the year. She has been married to Bern for 5 years; he works as a PE Teacher at a local comprehensive school. Sienna undertook her degree at Cardiff University in 2000 in English Literature. She is a great mother and really enjoys her work.

Max Jones:

Max has two years' experience of being a Customer Service Manager at the High Street Bank's Midshire Branch. Prior to that he worked in customer services in the same bank. Like Sienna, he is applying for the part-time role as he wants to improve his work life balance and spend more time with his children, twin boys, Chris and Nick, aged two. He has been married to Gill for 10 years and she works in Academia. He is well liked by his team and his colleagues and repeatedly receives good feedback from both his managers and customers. He graduated from University of Portsmouth in 1997 with a degree in History. He is a very dedicated dad as well as getting a lot of satisfaction from work.

Following on from this task, they were then asked to rate the full-time applicants and were informed:

Both your part-time members of staff have left, and you now have a vacancy for a full-time position (37.5 hours per week) for a Customer Services Manager (same role summary applies). As before, please read these two summaries of job applicants and then individually rate each applicant.

Amelia Smith:

Amelia has been Deputy Manager of the Customer Services Team at The National Bank for 7 years. She worked her way up from the role of Receptionist at the same bank that she joined upon graduation from Sheffield University where she studied Communications. She has a proven track record of success at the National Bank with good performance management ratings from her peers, managers, subordinates and customers. She is applying for the role as she thinks it will be interesting and she likes to provide a good life for her family – husband James, a school caretaker and children, Katherine and James (Aged 2 and 6 months). Amelia says she loves being a working mum.

Oliver Williams:

Oliver is an internal applicant who has been working as the "acting" Customer Service Manager at High Street Bank for the last 6 months. He joined High Street bank after graduating in Business from Liverpool University and has held numerous jobs at the bank since then. His team won a recent award for customer service, voted for by Customers. He is married to Clare who is a university administrator and has two children, Justine and Bethany (Aged 3 and 1). He is applying for the job to give his children and wife a better standard of living and being a working dad is important to him.

The sample of manager participants comprised 64 men and 33 women, with four participants not specifying their gender. A detailed analysis of Co-Variance (ANCOVA) approach was taken. ANCOVA was utilised by Berdahl and Moon (2013) in a very similar study; therefore, it seemed highly appropriate to follow their choice of analysis. The main experimental manipulation and dependent variables for the analysis were 'Applicant Ratings', against the measures of 'workplace commitment', 'hireability', 'promotability' and 'perceived competence'. It was also necessary to analyse the impact of 'Applicant Working Hours' (part-time/full-time) and 'Gender of the Applicant' (mother/father) and ascertain whether or not these covariates impacted on the dependent variable of 'Applicant Ratings'. Therefore, the independent variables were full-time mother applicant, full-time father applicant, part-time father applicant and part-time mother applicant.

Whilst some capacity for data analysis exists within Qualtrics, the Statistical Package for the Social Sciences (SPSS—2015 Version) software was employed due to its wider capability, specifically with regard to the production of tables and visual representations (Anderson et al., 2007).

As the gender of participants in the sample was uneven, the potential impact of this was tested using multivariate between-subjects testing. It was found that there were no significant interactions between the 'Gender of Applicant', 'Applicant Working Hours' and 'Gender of Participant' which thus provided confidence that the analysis was not impacted upon by the dominance of male participants.

The initial descriptive statistics of the online vignette survey element of the 'Fatherhood Forfeit Study' (see Table 2.1) indicated that the caregiving father applicant, depicted as an applicant for a part-time role, was rated lower than the part-time mother applicant, and both the parent applicants for the full-time role across all dependent variables ('workplace commitment', 'hireability', 'promotability' and 'perceived competence'). The largest difference in the ratings between applicants was evident with regard to the variable of 'perceived competence'. Additionally, it is observable

Table 2.1 Detailed descriptive statistics-mean scores

	Part-time applicant		Full-time applicant	
	Father	Mother	Father	Mother
Promotability	6.94	7.49 (0.55)	7.78	7.87 (0.09)
Hireability	7.76	8.49 (0.73)	7.77	8.07 (0.3)
Workplace commitment	7.46	7.73 (0.27)	7.94	8.16 (0.22)
Perceived competence	7.44	8.46 (1.02)	7.82	7.88 (0.06)
Total	29.6	32.17 (2.57)	31.31	31.98 (0.67)

that the part-time father applicant was judged more harshly than the other working parent scenarios with regard to the dependent variable of 'promotability'. These non-statistically robust results imply that gender is a factor when rating applicants, and that whether an applicant is a mother or a father and applying for part-time or full-time work appears to have an impact upon how they are rated; thus, a more detailed analysis was undertaken.

The next part of the analysis involved the more statistically robust type of ANCOVA testing, employing multivariate analysis with a within-subject test.

The within-subject test exposed two significant differences in the mean scores that are central to the research presented in this book. Firstly, statistical significance was found in the differences between the means of 'Gender of Applicant' (mother/father) and 'Applicant Ratings' (F (4. 77) = 10.019, P = 0.00). Secondly, a significant difference can be observed with regard to the 'Applicant Working Hours' (whether part-time or full-time) and the 'Applicant Ratings' (F (4.77) = 6.460, P = 0.00). This suggests that mothers and fathers are rated differently when applying for part-time and full-time roles, with 'Gender of Applicant' (mother or father) and 'Applicant Working Hours' (working full-time or part-time) affecting how they are rated.

With this established, it was necessary to delve more deeply into the analysis to explore whether any statistically significant differences exist between how applicants were rated against the specific measures of 'promotability', 'hireability', 'workplace commitment' and 'perceived competence' through exploration of the estimated marginal means (EMM) section of the SPSS output which can be useful in determining the nature of the established interaction (Field, 2009). The differences in profile plots are highlighted below and are used to establish in detail how the parent applicants were rated when they applied for the fictitious part-time or full-time role and how the ratings compare to each other.

'PROMOTABILITY'

With regard to promotability, it is evident that the part-time father applicant was rated the lowest out of all four applicants: part-time (mother), part-time (father), full-time (mother), full-time (father). The effect was present for both the full-time and part-time parent applicants, with the strongest difference being observable between the mother and father applicants for the part-time position.

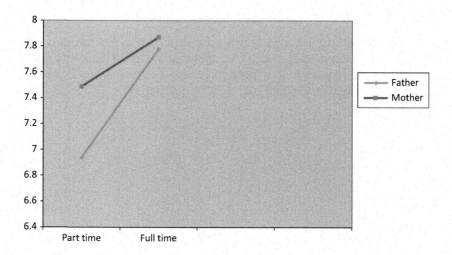

'Hireability'

The dependent variable of 'hireability' (below) shows a slightly different pattern to that of 'promotability'. Whilst the part-time father was still rated lower than the part-time and full-time mother against the criteria of 'hireability', there was only a slight difference between the ratings of 'hireability' for the part-time and full-time father.

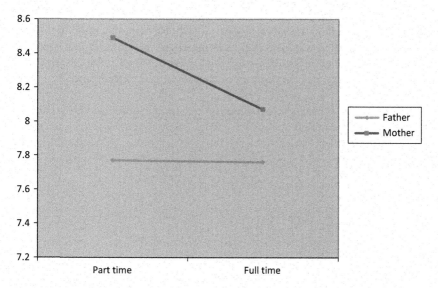

'WORKPLACE COMMITMENT'

The analysis of responses against the criteria of 'workplace commitment' demonstrates that the part-time father applicant was again the lowest rated of all of the applicants. It is observable that both full-time applicants scored more highly than their part-time counterparts.

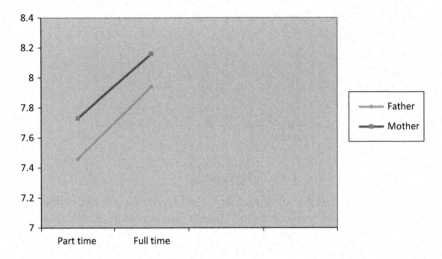

'PERCEIVED COMPETENCE'

The last dependent variable against which participants rated fictitious applicant vignettes was 'perceived competence'. It is observable that the part-time father applicant obtained the lowest score with the greatest disparity being between the ratings of the part-time mother and the part-time father applicant, with a more marginal difference between the rating of 'perceived competence' between the full-time mother and father applicant being observable.

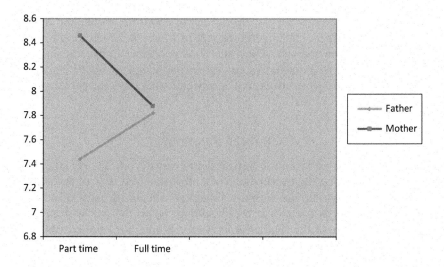

To conclude, the analysis of the EMM demonstrated that for each of the dependent variables ('promotability', 'hireability', 'workplace commitment' and 'perceived competence'), the part-time father applicant obtained the lowest rating, and although the extent of this varied, a lower score was consistent.

THE FATHERHOOD FORFEIT

The data that arose from the online vignette survey part of the 'Fatherhood Forfeit Study' point to a difference in the rating of the caregiving father, represented as a father applying for a part-time role, compared to the ratings of the mother applying for a part-time role, and mother and father applicants for the full-time role. Thus, it is suggested that caregiving fathers face a 'fatherhood forfeit' when they try to combine work and caregiving. That is to say they are less likely to obtain a role that would help them manage the dual responsibilities of family and work than mothers who were trying to do the same.

The notion of caregiving fathers facing 'fatherhood forfeits' is the central premise of this book and will continue to be explored in the later chapters. Such quantitative findings demonstrate differences in the way in which parents are rated when applying for job roles that facilitate caregiving; however, these data do not tell us about the nature and ratio-nale for this decision-making and the way in which the fatherhood forfeit manifests in the workplace. Thus, the book continues to present further data which deployed qualitative insights through vignette-based manager focus groups and semi-structured interviews with working parents and managers.

Chapter Summary

This chapter has explored the historical context of work, society and par-enthood, outlining the expectations of a more involved style of parenting for contemporary fathers within a lingering climate of expectations of alignment towards traditional breadwinning norms. The data from the quantitative part of the 'Fatherhood Forfeit Study' were presented, and the notion of 'fatherhood forfeits' was introduced. It was identified that data from the quantitative element of the 'Fatherhood Forfeit Study' found that the caregiving father in the vignette survey, represented as a part-time applicant, was rated lower than other working parents when applying for a role conducive to caregiving. Thus, fathers were observed to be less likely to obtain a role that allows them to combine caregiving and work (such as part-time employment) due to scoring lower than their counterparts at the point of shortlisting.

The following chapters explore the notion of 'fatherhood forfeits' in more depth through further investigation of both literature and empirical data. Specifically, they focus on uncovering what might lie behind the dis-criminatory decisions that managers made in the quantitative part of the 'Fatherhood Forfeit Study' outlined within this chapter and indicate how such perceptions of caregiving fathers might have a part to play in the prevailing dominance of the breadwinner model despite a position of pur-ported increased gender equality for working parents.

References

Allard, K., Haas, L., & Hwang, C. P. (2011). Family-supportive organizational culture and fathers' experiences of work–family conflict in Sweden. *Gender, Work and Organization, 18*(2), 141–157. https://doi.org/10.1111/j.1468-0432.2010.00540.x

Anderson, D. R., Sweeney, D. J., & Williams-Rochester, T. J. (2007). *Statistics for business and economics* (9th ed.). Thomson Press (India) Ltd.

Aumann, K., Galinsky, E., & Matos, K. (2011). *The new male mystique* (National study of the changing workforce). Families and Work Institute. Available at: http://familiesandwork.org/site/research/reports/newmalemystique.pdf. Accessed 28 Sept 2018.

Barnett, R. C. & Hyde, J. S. (2001). Women, men, work and family: An expansionist theory. *American Psychologist, 56*(10), pp. 781–796. https://doi.org/10.1037/0003-066X.56.10.781

Barnhoorn, J. S., Haasnoot, E., Bocanegra, B. R., & van Steenbergen, H. (2015). QRT Engine: An easy solution for running online reaction time experiments using Qualtrics. *Behavior Research Methods, 47*(4), 918–929. https://doi.org/10.3758/s13428-014-0530-7

Berdahl, J. L., & Moon, S. H. (2013). Workplace mistreatment of middle class workers based on sex, parenthood and caregiving. *Journal of Social Issues, 69*(2), 341–366. https://doi.org/10.1111/josi.12018

Berghammer, C. (2014). The return of the male breadwinner model? Educational effects on parents' work arrangements in Austria, 1980–2009. *Work, Employment and Society, 28*(4), 611–632. https://doi.org/10.1177/0950017013500115

Bergman, H., & Hobson, B. (2002). Compulsory fatherhood: The coding of fatherhood in the Swedish Welfare State. In B. Hobson (Ed.), *Making men into fathers: Men, masculinities and the social politics of fatherhood* (pp. 92–125). Cambridge University Press.

Besen, Y. (2007). Masculinities at work. *Equal Opportunities International, 26*(3), 256–260. https://doi.org/10.1108/02610150710735534

Bland, L. (2005). White women and men of colour: Miscegenation fears in Britain after the Great War. *Gender & History, 17*(1), 29–61. https://doi.org/10.1111/j.0953-5233.2005.00371.x

Brannen, J., & Nilsen, A. (2006). From fatherhood to fathering; transmission and change among British fathers in four generation families. *Sociology, 40*(2), 335–352.

Broughton, T. L., & Rogers, H. (Eds.). (2007). *Gender and fatherhood in the nineteenth century.* Palgrave Macmillan.

Bryman, A., & Bell, E. (2011). *Business research methods* (3rd ed.). Oxford University Press.

Budworth, M., Enns, J., & Rowbotham, K. (2008). Shared identity and strategic choice in dual career couples. *Gender in Management: An International Journal, 23*(2), 103–119. https://doi.org/10.1108/17542410810858312

Burke, R. J., & Onwuegbuzie, A. J. (2004). Mixed methods research: A research paradigm whose time has come. *Educational Researcher, 33*(7), 14–26. https://doi.org/10.3102/0013189X033007014

Burnett, S. B., Gatrell, C. J., Cooper, C. L., & Sparrow, P. (2010). Well balanced families? A gendered analysis of work–life balance policies and work family practices. *International Journal of Gender in Management, 25*(7), 534–549. Available at: https://www.researchgate.net/publication/235253790_Well-balanced_families_A_gendered_analysis_of_work-life_balance_policies_and_work_family_practices. Accessed 28 Sept 2018.

Burnett, S. B., Gatrell, C. J., Cooper, C. L., & Sparrow, P. (2013). Fathers at work: A ghost in the organizational machine. *Gender, Work & Organization, 20*(6), pp. 632–646. https://doi.org/10.1111/gwao.12000

Cabrera, N., Tamis-LeMonda, C. S., Bradley, R. H., Hofferth, S., & Lamb, M. E. (2000). Fatherhood in the twenty-first century. *Child Development, 71*(1), 127–136.

Carr-Ruffino, N. (1993). *The promotable woman*. Van Nostrand.

Collis, J., & Hussey, R. (2013). *Business research: A practical guide for undergraduate and postgraduate students* (4th ed.). Palgrave Macmillan.

Correll, S., Benard, S., & Paik, I. (2007). Getting a job: Is there a motherhood penalty? *American Journal of Sociology, 112*(5), 1297–1338.

Crompton, R. (2002). Employment, flexible working and the family. *British Journal of Sociology, 53*(4), 537–558.

Cuddy, A. C., Fiske, S. T., & Glick, P. (2004). When professionals become mothers, warmth doesn't cut the ice. *Journal of Social Issues, 60*(4), 701–718. https://doi.org/10.1111/j.0022-4537.2004.00381.x

Department for Business, Innovation and Skills. (2013). *Workplace Employment Relations Study (2011)*. Available at: https://www.gov.uk/government/publications/the-2011-workplace-employment-relations-study-wers. Accessed 28 Sept 2018.

Dermott, E. (2008). *Intimate fatherhood: A sociological analysis*. Routledge.

EHRC. (2009). *Working better: Fathers, family and work – Contemporary perspectives* (Research summary 41). Equality and Human Rights Commission. Available at: https://www.equalityhumanrights.com/en/publication-download/research-summary-41-working-better-fathers-family-and-work-contemporary. Accessed 28 Sept 2018.

Eikhof, D. (2012). A double edged sword; twenty first century workplace trends and gender equality. *Gender in Management: An International Journal, 27*(1), 7–22.

Elder, G. H., Jr. (1998). *Children of the great depression: Social change in life experience* (25th anniversary ed.). Westview Press.

Fevre, R., Robinson, A., Jones, T., & Lewis, D. (2010). Researching workplace bullying: The benefits of taking an integrated approach. *International Journal of Social Research Methodology, 13*(1), 71–85.

Field, A. (2009). *Discovering statistics using SPSS. Thousand Oaks*. California: Sage Publications.

Fuegen, K., Biernat, M., Haines, E., & Deaux, K. (2004). Mothers and fathers in the workplace: How gender and parental status influence judgments of job-related competence. *Journal of Social Issues, 60*(4), 737–754.

Ganong, L. H., & Coleman, M. (2006). Multiple segment factorial vignette designs. *Journal of Marriage and Family, 68*(2), 455–468.

Gatrell, C. J., Burnett, S. B., Cooper, C. L., & Sparrow, P. (2014). Parents, perceptions and belonging: Exploring flexible working among UK fathers and mothers. *British Journal of Management, 25*(3), 473–487.

Gillis, J. (2000). Marginalisation of fatherhood in Western countries. *Childhood, 17*(2), 225–238.

Graham, C. R. (2011). Theoretical considerations for understanding technological pedagogical content knowledge (TPACK). *Com[1]puters & Education, 57*, 1953–1960.

Halford, S. (2006). Collapsing the boundaries? Fatherhood, organization and home-working. *Gender, Work and Organization, 13*(4), 383–402.

Hilbrecht, M., Shaw, S. M., Johnson, L. C., & Andrey, J. (2008). I'm home for the kids – Contradictory implications for work life balance of teleworking mothers. *Gender, Work and Organisation, 15*(5), 454–476.

Holter, O. (2007). Men's work and family reconciliation in Europe. *Men and Masculinities, 9*(4), 425–456.

Howe, D. (2011). *Attachment across the lifecourse: A brief introduction.* Macmillan International Higher Education.

Karpinska, K., Henkens, K., & Schippers, J. (2011). The recruitment of early retirees: A vignette study of the factors that affect managers' decisions. *Ageing and Society, 31*(4), 570–589. https://doi.org/10.1017/S0144686X10001078

Lamb, M. E. (2008). The history of research on father involvement. *Marriage & Family Review, 29*(2–3), 23–42. https://doi.org/10.1300/J002v29n02_03

Lewis, D., Hoel, H., & Einarsdottir, A. (2013). *Hard to research and hard to reach: Methodological challenges in exploring bullying, harassment and discrimination with lesbian, gay and bisexual employees.* 13th EURAM conference, Istanbul, 26–29th June.

Light, J. S. (1999). When computers were women. *Technology and Culture, 40*(3), 455–483.

Matthews, K. A., & Rodin, J. (1989). Women's changing work roles: Impact on health, family, and public policy. *American Psychologist, 44*(11), 1389–1393.

Maund, L. (2001). *An introduction to human resource management.* Palgrave.

Maylor, H. and Blackmon, K. (2005) 'Chapter 5: Scientist or ethnographer: Two models for designing and doing research', in Maylor, H. and Blackmon, K., Researching business and management. Palgrave Macmillan, pp. 134-164.

Miles, M. B., & Huberman, A. M. (1994). *Qualitative data analysis: An expanded sourcebook.* Sage.

National Child Development Study. (2008). *Now we are 50. Key findings from the National child development study.* J. Elliott & R. Vaitilingam (Eds.). Available at: https://ncds.info/resources/ Accessed 28 Sept 2018.

Norman, H. (2010). *Involved fatherhood: An analysis of the conditions associated with paternal involvement in childcare and housework.* Unpublished doctoral thesis, University of Manchester. Available at: https://www.escholar.manchester.ac.uk/uk-ac-man-scw:163780

O'Brien, M. (2005). *Shared caring: Bringing fathers into the frame* (EOC Working Paper Series No. 18). Equal Opportunities Commission. Available at: http://dera.ioe.ac.uk/5299/1/1.73363%21shared_caring_wp18.pdf. Accessed 28 Sept 2018.

Office for National Statistics. (2011). *Impact of the recession.* Available at: http://webarchive.nationalarchives.gov.uk/20160113233720/http://www.ons.gov.uk/ons/dcp171766_240249.pdf. Accessed 28 Sept 2018.

Office for National Statistics. (2013). *Women in the labour market.* Available at: https://www.ons.gov.uk/employmentandlabourmarket/peopleinwork/employmentandemployeetypes/articles/womeninthelabourmarket/2013-09-25. Accessed 28 Sept 2018.

Office for National Statistics. (2019). *Families in the labour market.* Available at: https://www.ons.gov.uk/employmentandlabourmarket/peopleinwork/employmentandemployeetypes/articles/familiesandthelabourmarketengland/2019. Accessed 8 Nov 2021.

Perrons, D. (2009). Gender and social policy in a global context: Uncovering the gendered structure of the social. *Feminist Economics, 15*(1), 151–155.

Pleck, J. (1997). Paternal involvement: Levels, sources and consequences. In M. E. Lamb (Ed.), *The role of the father in child development* (3rd ed., pp. 66–103). Wiley.

Pleck, E. H., & Pleck, J. H. (1997). Fatherhood ideals in the United States: Historical dimensions. In M. E. Lamb (Ed.), *The role of the father in child development* (3rd ed., pp. 33–48). Wiley.

Pocock, B. (2005). Work/care regimes: institutions, culture and behaviour and the Australian case. *Gender, Work & Organization, 12*(1), pp. 32–49.

Podnieks, E. (Ed.). (2016). *Pops in pop culture* (pp. 1–27). Palgrave Macmillan.

Powell, C. (2021, November). Use of shared parental leave dropped 17 per cent during Covid. *People Management Magazine.* Available at: https://www.peoplemanagement.co.uk/news/articles/use-shared-parental-leave-dropped-17-per-cent-during-covid-study-finds#gref Accessed 8 Nov 2021.

Probert, B. (2005). 'I just couldn't fit it in': Gender and unequal outcomes in academic careers. *Gender, Work and Organization, 12*(1), 50–72. https://doi.org/10.1111/j.1468-0432.2005.00262.x

Rossi, P. H., & Anderson, A. B. (1982). The factorial survey approach: An introduction. In *Measuring social judgments: The factorial survey approach* (pp. 15–67).

Sarantakos, S. (2005). *Social research* (3rd ed.). Palgrave Macmillan.
Saunders, M., Lewis, P., & Thornhill, A. (2007). *Research methods for business students* (4th ed.). Prentice Hall.
Shows, C., & Gerstel, N. (2009). Fathering, class, and gender: A comparison of physicians and emergency medical technicians. *Gender & Society, 23*(2), 161–187. https://doi.org/10.1177/0891243209333872
Skeels, M. M., & Grudin, J. (2009, May). When social networks cross boundaries: A case study of workplace use of Facebook and LinkedIn. In *Proceedings of the ACM 2009 international conference on Supporting group work* (pp. 95–104).
Smith, J. (1995). The first intruder: Fatherhood, a historical perspective. In P. Moss (Ed.), *Father figures: Fathers in the families of the 1990s.* HMSO.
Solomon, C. R. (2014). 'After months of it, you just want to punch someone in the face': Stay-at-home fathers and masculine identities. *Michigan Family Review, 18*(1), 23–38. https://doi.org/10.3998/mfr.4919087.0018.103
Stanworth, C. (2000). Women and work in the information age. *Gender, Work and Organization, 7*(1), 20–32.
Stuart, M., Grugulis, I., Tomlinson, J., Forde, C., & MacKenzie, R. (2013). Reflections on work and employment into the 21st century: Between equal rights, force decides. *Work, Employment and Society, 27*(3), 379–395. https://doi.org/10.1177/0950017013489615
Townsend, N. W. (2002). *The package deal: Marriage, work and fatherhood in men's lives.* Temple University Press.
Wallander, L. (2009). 25 years of factorial surveys in sociology: A review. *Social Science Research, 38*(3), 505–520.
Wang, W., Parker, K., & Taylor, P. (2013). *Breadwinner moms: Mothers are the sole or primary provider in four-in-ten households with children; public conflicted about the growing trend.* Pew Research Centre. Available at: http://www.pew-socialtrends.org/2013/05/29/breadwinner-moms/. Accessed 28 Sept 2018.
Wells, M. B., & Sarkadi, A. (2012). Do father-friendly policies promote father-friendly child-rearing practices? A review of Swedish parental leave and child health centers. *Journal of Child and Family Studies, 21*(1), 25–31. https://doi.org/10.1007/s10826-011-9487-7
Whittaker, A. (2009). *Research skills for social work.* Learning Matters Ltd.

CHAPTER 3

Parental Gender Stereotyping and 'Think Child–Think Mum'

Abstract This chapter begins by exploring the current literature surrounding parental gender stereotyping, offering explanations as to why mothers are often considered as the primary caregiving parent. It discusses gendered stereotypes in a general sense, their influence on norms of behaviour and then how this impacts on behavioural expectations within the workplace for parents, emphasising the differing expectations of mothers and fathers.

The chapter then moves on to present the qualitative data from the 'Fatherhood Forfeit Study' which comprised vignette-based manager focus groups and semi-structured interviews with working parents and managers. The emphasis in this chapter is on the overarching theme of 'Think-Child-Think-Mum'. Illustrative quotes are employed to explore the ways in which parent and manager participants make automatic assumptions regarding primary caregiving status through the sub-themes of 'Where is Mum?' and 'Unconventionality'. Throughout the chapter, the study data are linked to existing academic literature, outlining the ways in which the findings of the qualitative element of the 'Fatherhood Forfeit Study' both corresponds with and contradicts existing work.

Keywords Fathers • Discrimination • Gender Stereotypes • Breadwinner/Breadwinning • Unconventionality • Flexible working

© The Author(s), under exclusive license to Springer Nature Switzerland AG 2022
J. Kelland, *Caregiving Fathers in the Workplace*,
https://doi.org/10.1007/978-3-030-97971-3_3

GENDER STEREOTYPING

Existing literature is suggestive that the extent of parental involvement in caregiving has both a biological and social underpinning and offers explanations of why, for many families, the mother in the household spends more time caring for children than the father (Eagly, 1987; Wood & Eagly, 2002). Whilst there are undeniable biological differences between men and women, the extent of the 'nature' argument is debateable, with many theorists arguing that the unequal division of caregiving responsibilities is not a result of biological differences but may be more related to the social construction of gender roles (Giddens & Sutton, 2013). As such, the 'nurture' argument advocates that it is the reinforcement of expected gendered behaviour that impacts upon parental involvement in caregiving rather than any actual 'nature' differences per se.

Early theorists, such as Freud and Erikson, pointed to an establishment of disparities in gender roles emerging from childhood as a consequence of different early socialisation experiences underpinned by inherent biological differences (Freud, 1953; Erikson, 1968; Barnett & Hyde, 2001). Such social construction of gender roles has been observed to occur through stereotypes imposed by parents, teachers and peers during childhood in which the views of children are shaped by their environment and culture (Harkness & Super, 1995; Silverstein et al., 2002; Giddens & Sutton, 2013). Unsurprisingly, existing research findings are largely consistent with this view, implying that parents have a key role in influencing young children in regard to gendered behaviour (Kaplan, 1991; Santrock, 1994; Berryman-Fink et al., 2015).

It is proposed that from an early age, awareness exists of gender role differences, with children beginning to use gender stereotypes to navigate their world in relation to activities, objects and occupations (Biernat, 1991; Harkness & Super, 1995; Lobel et al., 2001). The gender role attitudes of children have been found to be significantly affected by their exposure to gendered behaviour through the actions of parents and the extent to which desired conduct is reinforced with approval or with disapproval and sanctions for deviation (Mischel, 1966; Santrock, 1994; Marks et al., 2009). Similarly, gender messages have been observed to be transmitted through differences in the treatment of sons and daughters and different expectations of behaviour dependent on gender, often involving influential inferences regarding gender acceptable behaviour (Witt, 2000).

Such purported differentials in treatment between boys and girls can manifest in many ways, including dressing in gender-specific colours, giving gender-specific toys, encouraging playing with dolls and housekeeping in girls and playing with trucks and engaging in sports activities in boys, along with rewarding gender aligned play behaviour (Carter, 1987; Eccles et al., 1990; Thorne, 1993). Moreover, for girls it has been found that there is an expectation that they will be nurturing, deferential and passive, whereas boys have been found to be expected to be autonomous, aggressive, dominant and achievement oriented (Beloff, 1992; Lobel, 1994; Nadler & Stockdale, 2012). With regard to work and family, it has been found that as children get slightly older and attend school some will develop a sense that it is unacceptable for fathers to stay home to take a lead role in caregiving and that mothers are better parents (Eccles, 1983; Sinno & Killen, 2009).

Naturally, such childhood stereotyping can have a long-term impact on caregiving activities when children grow up and become parents themselves with parental division of labour during childhood suggested to be a key indicator of adult behaviours (Cunningham, 2001). Boys assigned non-gender-stereotyped tasks during their childhood have been found to be more likely to have a higher level of involvement with their own children than boys who were allocated more gender stereotypical duties (Gerson, 1993; Pleck & Pleck, 1997). Similarly, boys with involved fathers are more likely to be involved with their own children, display gender equality in their behaviour with their own children, and also their daughters are likely to have higher career aspirations than those with fathers who were less involved (Hofferth, 1999; Croft et al., 2014; Levtov et al., 2015).

As children grow up, research indicates that women are expected to be socially sensitive, communal, nurturing, co-operative, intuitive, emotional and empathic. Whereas men are associated with being independent, competitive, logical, rational, strategic, assertive and achievement-oriented, with rewards received for alignment to such stereotypes for both men and women (Carr-Ruffino, 1993; Sheridan, 2004; Heilman & Wallen, 2010; Giddens & Sutton, 2013). Further, according to notions of 'prescriptive gender bias', individuals expect to be perceived and evaluated differently depending on whether their actions violate expectations of how they should act (Luzadis et al., 2008; Eagly & Karau, 2002).

GENDER STEREOTYPING AT WORK

When applied to an organisational setting, gender stereotyping can be observed to dictate behavioural norms specifying both the "shoulds" and the "should nots" of workplace behaviour (Heilman, 2001; Eagly & Karau, 2002; Heilman & Parks-Stamm, 2007; Heilman & Wallen, 2010: 664). This can be observed to translate into the occupational sex typing of job roles which is a mechanism for describing how some occupations are associated with a certain sex, and that only this coupling will be considered to be 'normal' and 'natural' (Collinson et al., 1990). Theorists of sex typing propose that due to stereotypical gender 'traits', one gender is considered not to have the skills needed to perform the role of the other, with many professions categorised as appropriate or suitable for a certain gender (Padavic & Reskin, 2002; Holmes, 2006; Kelan, 2010).

Feminised workplaces have been observed to be characterised by the stereotypical features of femininity such as caring, supportive, person-orientated and often involving 'front-line' activities (such as nursing), whilst other 'central' activities (such as maintenance) are often performed by men (Broadbridge & Hearn, 2008). Some of the strongest impact regarding occupational sex typing can be observed with regard to the assumed more masculine occupations (such as engineering) in which women are believed to be less likely to be successful in the role due to deep-rooted beliefs grounded in gendered stereotypes (Collinson, 1988; Eagly & Koenig, 2008). Sex typing can occur early in the employment relationship, and it is likely that a less qualified applicant who is aligned to the sex typing of the job would be hired, with interviewers preferring applicants whose gender is aligned to the occupational sex typing (Atwater & Van Fleet, 1997; Noon, 2012). Deviations from roles that can be viewed as having aligned prescriptive stereotypes, such as male nurses and female engineers, have been found to be more likely to result in negative evaluation than someone who is in a more gender-consistent role (Luzadis et al., 2008; Eagly & Karau, 2002). This affect is observable for both sexes, with men and women being found to receive negative reactions when behaving in a way that is inconsistent with gendered stereotypes (Flynn & Ames, 2006; Heilman & Wallen, 2010; Moss-Racusin et al., 2012). Pertinent to the focus of this book, male applicants have been found to be discriminated against for jobs that are considered feminine or 'female work' and can be negatively affected due to what is described as the 'women-are-wonderful effect' (Glick et al., 1988; Eagly & Mladinic, 1989; Atwater & Van Fleet, 1997; Langford & MacKinnon, 2000). Both men and women in gender-inconsistent roles have been found to face social and economic penalties, and these 'backlash effects' can result in some individuals being 'marked', seen as deviant, and in some way separate from the mainstream (Rudman & Phelan, 2008; Baxter, 2010; Ku, 2011). Such stereotyping has traditionally been associated with having a detrimental effect on mothers in the workplace; however, more recently, this has been observed to be faced by fathers when they act in a non-stereotypical manner by undertaking caregiving activities (Correll & Ridgeway, 2006; Correll et al., 2007; Berdahl & Moon, 2013). The 'Fatherhood Forfeit Study' specifically explored the issue of gender stereotyping through the qualitative data collection, and these data will now be presented with key findings and associations with existing literature outlined.

FATHERHOOD FORFEIT STUDY: VIGNETTE-BASED FOCUS GROUPS AND SEMI-STRUCTURED INTERVIEWS

The online vignette survey element of the 'Fatherhood Forfeit Study' demonstrated that the caregiving father, represented as a part-time applicant, was consistently rated lower than the other working parent scenarios and thus they were less likely to obtain a role to facilitate caregiving. However, due to its quantitative nature, the online vignette survey element of the 'Fatherhood Forfeit Study' did not explore potential rationales for such discriminatory decision making. Thus, this chapter explores the qualitative data from the vignette-based manager focus groups and semi-structured interviews with managers and working parents, seeking to provide insights into the ratings given to the caregiving father, represented as a part-time father applicant in the online vignette and the workplace perceptions of caregiving fathers and their experiences more generally.

Focus groups are a popular research method (Anderson, 2009), particularly those based on vignettes (Beaulieu et al., 1999). On a practical level, this method has the benefit of being able to reach a large number of participants in a relatively short space of time (Kamberelis and Dimitriadis in Denzin & Lincoln, 2017) and is considered to be less prone to bias and subjectivity than some of the other available research methods (Howell,

2013). On a more theoretical level, focus groups enable the collection of opinions regarding a topic, enabling views to be explored with other participants, resulting in "powerful interpretive insights", that incorporate both content and expression as a result of creating a social interaction (Whittaker, 2009; Kamberelis and Dimitriadis in Denzin & Lincoln, 2017: 903). Focus groups also have the capacity to expose "unarticulated norms and normative assumptions" which is particularly pertinent for this study presented within this book (Kamberelis and Dimitriadis, in Denzin & Lincoln, 2017: 903). It is important to note that focus groups are not without their limitations. In particular, group dynamics can result in the powerful, extrovert, members overtaking the discussion so less confident participants have only minimal contribution (Whittaker, 2009). The researcher was mindful of this during the vignette-based focus groups and ensured that they intervened when necessary to encourage equal participant contributions. The participants for the vignette-based focus groups were obtained through direct requests to human resource managers via email. As with the online vignette, in order to maximise the likelihood that the study would be an accurate reflection of workplace practices the prerequisite of participation was that participants needed to be a manager with experience of recruitment and selection. Eleven HR managers were contacted regarding the participation of their managers and four HR managers agreed for their organisations to participate. The vignette-based focus groups were all run in situ and the organisations comprised the charity sector, technology, NHS and Naval (two focus groups).

The vignette-based focus groups provided some understanding regarding what lies behind the ratings allocated in the online vignette survey and began to create a sense of how caregiving fathers are perceived in contemporary workplaces. However, in order to fully understand the perceptions and experiences of caregiving fathers, it was necessary to gather wider data from managers and parents; thus semi-structured interviews were also utilised as a method. The semi-structured interview has been described as the "gold standard of qualitative research" (Silverman, 2000: 291) resulting in high-quality information (Whittaker, 2009). These have the key benefit of allowing the researcher to access information through probing for more detailed responses and thus obtain the "complete story" from the respondents through the establishment of structure, whilst permitting exploration of topics of particular interest (Leidner, 1993; Sheppard, 2004: 149; Whittaker, 2009). The semi-structured interviews were normally undertaken face to face, but occasionally via telephone due to participant availability or preference. The participants for the semi-structured interviews were drawn from a number of different populations, including some participants responding to a direct request from the researcher (via email or LinkedIn) and others indicating a willingness to participate after undertaking the vignette-based focus groups or online vignette. The only prerequisite for participation in the semi-structured interviews was that participants needed to be either a manager or a working parent. Experience in recruitment and selection was not essential for this part of the study as it was concerned with broadly held experiences and perceptions of caregiving fathers that would be unaffected by lack of experience of recruitment and selection. It was envisaged that by having minimal prerequisites, there would be a wide variation in participants, which would result in the emerging data being largely representative of the population, enabling generalisations and predictions from the data (Howell, 2013).

All transcripts were reviewed for accuracy by the researcher prior to initial coding. Each transcription was read and re-read in detail which enabled the researcher to become thoroughly familiar with the data and develop an in-depth understanding of them, This is particularly important when analysing qualitative data (Perakyla in Denzin & Lincoln, 2005; Hammersley & Atkinson, 2007).

Coding Process

In order to analyse the collected qualitative data it was necessary to first categorise the data to enable its management, identifying themes and patterns (Howell, 2013). To this end the coding process was divided into four phases to underpin the qualitative analysis, creating an "analytic scaffolding on which to build" (Charmaz, in Denzin & Lincoln, 2005: 517). The findings presented here emerged from a four-stage thematic analysis process (Braun & Clarke, 2006), involving initial line-by-line analysis, a data reduction process, preliminary coding and then a final development of key codes (Miles & Huberman, 1994; Charmaz, in Denzin & Lincoln, 2005). Phase one began after the researcher was confident that the transcripts were accurate and involved line-by-line coding, seeking codes that had already been identified within the literature and aligning them to the research aim. This "start list" (Miles & Huberman, 1994: 58) utilised broad codes to encompass any areas, which might potentially be of interest to the researcher; essentially, any reference to workplace perceptions or experiences of fathers within the workplace. Phase two involved re-reading the transcripts, highlighting and removing any data that were not relevant by way of data reduction (Miles & Huberman, 1994). Once again, central to this process was alignment to the purposes of the research, which included highlighting specific areas of workplace treatment of fathers who were attempting to amend their working patterns due to caregiving responsibilities. During phase three, the reduced transcripts were read again and the researcher began to group together the statements with regard to the workplace treatment of caregiving fathers. This preliminary coding resulted in over 20 codes, which represented emerging concepts with regard to the workplace treatment of caregiving fathers (Miles & Huberman, 1994). Phase four of the coding involved revising the codes, which included removing some codes and adding many sub-codes to allow for deeper analysis (Miles & Huberman, 1994). This level of coding involved an emphasis being placed on the codes which appeared most frequently, were discussed in depth by participants and aligned most closely to the purpose of the study. As a consequence, not all codes that emerged were used in the final analysis. This process was continued until the researcher felt that the scrutiny of the data had reached a saturation point, and regularities had started to emerge (Lincoln & Guba, 1985). The final codes that emerged from phase four were categorised into three main themes and identified as 'fatherhood forfeits'; 'Think Child–Think Mum', 'Fathers obtain less workplace support than mothers for caregiving' and 'Social Mistreatment of Caregiving Fathers'. Whilst it is believed this process was effective and undertaken in a robust manner, this approach can be described as selective, as the researcher consistently made the choice about what is pertinent and what is not (Miles & Huberman, 1994).

The sample for the qualitative element of the study comprised 27 manager focus group participants (10 female/17 male), 25 semi-structured interviews with working parents (12 fathers/13 mothers) and 15 managers (12 females/3 males). This chapter focuses on the theme of 'Think Child–Think Mum' which aligns closely to earlier discussions of the gender stereotyping literature, and the remaining themes will be explored in Chaps. 4 and 5. 'Think Child–Think Mum' is a phrase that has been employed to encompass a phenomenon that emerged frequently in the data, whereby the default caregiver for children is assumed to be the mother which is consistent with existing literature that supports the existence of parental gender role stereotyping.

'THINK CHILD–THINK MUM'

The theme of 'Think Child–Think Mum' was widely evident within the data, with both working parent and manager participants making statements which were demonstrative that parental responsibilities were primarily associated with mothers rather than fathers.

When managers discussed making recruitment decisions, the parental responsibilities of mothers appeared to be at the forefront of discussions, as illustrated by Sam, a NHS manager, who provided insight into her thought process when she interviewed a mother for a full-time role:

> We had an older manager who was going for a full-time job. She's a single mum with a two-year-old and I was very honest with her because I said, 'This is a full-time job, so would you manage that … there isn't any leeway in terms of, you know, breaking down to three days or four days; this is a full-time job on a ward, really busy.

When asked if she would have the same concerns about recruiting a father, her response was: "No, not so much. No". Further, she stated that if she was interviewing a father her thought process would be different, thus illustrating how mothers were associated with children in a way that fathers were not to the same degree. She continued:

> I've appointed lots of young people and you know whatever, who might not have children and stuff like that, but if you've got somebody who's over childbearing age you go, 'phew, well they're not going to go off on maternity leave'.

This was echoed by Amy, a team leader who stated that when recruiting a mother for a full-time position, her family circumstances would be of interest to managers:

> I think in their heads they would be having an internal discussion with themselves about how's this going to work … who else is around to care? So, I think you'd … maybe trying to pick up a few cues about the arrangements, but obviously, that can't be discussed, so I think I would be thinking, 'Okay, that sounds good. I wonder what's happening in the home then. Who picks up the pieces?' But I don't think you can really ask that so it is a little bit of informal.

Whereas, when asked if similar internal debates about managing caregiving responsibilities would occur for a father, the response, as with Sammi, was, "No. No". Similarly, Jenny, an HR and operations manager, stated:

> Women are seen as the caregivers, aren't they? So if there's anything that comes to children, it will be the mother that will have to sort things out. … day to day perceptions are that a man will work full-time and won't have family commitments … if you recruit a woman of a certain age, you kind of think they might be at marrying age and once they get married they're gonna have children, and if you've got a department of similar age woman some people do have cause for concern. Completely wrong, but I think that this is a factor.

Caren, a line manager, supports the notion that fathers are not automatically associated with children in the way that mothers are and illustrates how this manifests itself during the selection process:

> I don't think you would ever ask a man if he had children at home like a woman … I don't think anybody ever expects a father to give up time off work to look after the child. It just doesn't happen, does it? It doesn't happen. So, I don't think you would even think about it, and I doubt they ask.

This effect is also evident once in employment, as illustrated by Helen, a manager in a recruitment agency, who stated:

> It is most widely acknowledged and accepted that … mothers in the workplace may have higher absence than other employees because they have got caring responsibilities.

Therefore, fathers who are applying for part-time roles to allow for caregiving can be conceptualised as challenging this automatic 'Think Mum–Think Child' association. This might, in part, explain the ratings of the caregiving father, represented as a part-time father applicant, in the online vignette survey introduced in Chap. 2 and may help to explain the continued association of fathers with the role of breadwinner for their families.

Conversations within the vignette-based focus groups exploring applicant suitability are also indicative of the centrality of motherhood in this debate, whereas, for men, fatherhood rarely featured as a point of noteworthy discussion. When exploring the suitability of the mother applicants (both part and full-time), the following phrases were commonly used:

- "She might have been trying to have a baby".
- "She might have been thinking about moving up but then children come along".
- "Her children are young, it must have been hard working full-time".
- "She must have only recently come back to work because the youngest is only six months old".

When discussing the suitability of the father applicants (both part and full-time), parental status was not discussed in the way it had been for the mother applicants. Instead, debates focused on more general discussions regarding suitability against job criteria, such as:

- "He has got a degree"
- "I saw him as a utility person that is why he is acting now".
- "He is local".
- "He worked in customer services before he became a customer services manager".
- "He is in the place at the moment, he has been there for two years, so he has probably got job role experience".

Once again, it emerged that for parents in the workplace, there appears to be a default association between caregiving and mothers, with discussions on suitability being intertwined with an exploration of issues related to motherhood status. Whereas for fathers such an association did not emerge and discussions regarding suitability were focused on job-related criteria. This is in line with the observations of Sheridan (2004), who noted that men are associated with the stereotype of breadwinning, whereas the stereotypes regarding women focus on homemaking. Whilst this can be construed as giving fathers a workplace advantage in line with conceptualisations of 'fatherhood benefits' this appears to be dependent on the maintenance of a traditional gender ideology through full-time work (Correll et al., 2007; Berdahl & Moon, 2013). For fathers with caregiving responsibilities, such a lack of acknowledgement of their role as fathers might explain the lower ratings given to the caregiving father in the online vignette survey. Similarly, it might offer a partial explanation why so many fathers remain in breadwinning patterns of employment rather than working arrangements which are more conducive to caregiving. The overarching theme of 'Think Child–Think Mum' was also evident in interviews with working parents;

> (if a child was sick) it was probably 70/30 the expectation that I would drop everything to look after the children; 30 being my husband. (Luby, a married mother of two, both parents work full-time)

> If the children are sick, the first call is to Nicola (wife) ... If the school couldn't get hold of her they would call me. (David, a father of three, he works full-time his wife works part-time)

> I think as a mother, you're almost expected ... to have to go when your child is sick ... It never feels that the dads have that. When my husband worked in the bank it was always 'well you will have to do that', and I would say 'well, why have I got to do it', you are the Dad as well. (Stephanie, a married mother of two children, she works full-time and her husband work flexibly)

Such automatic assumptions that associate mothers with children can be conceptualised as presenting a challenge to fathers who have caregiving responsibilities. As illustrated by Paul and Rick:

> When I have told people that I am a single dad, they are like, 'you have a child' but I am actually his primary carer ... People still find that a little surprising, and I think there is always that assumption ... they think child [and] mother always go together. (Paul, a single father of one, works part-time)

> The mother goes to pick the children up from school, and the dad works long hours ... and, yes, it primarily was the male, and the female stayed at home for a variety of reasons. Many of my friends have chosen this, and their view was, 'Well, I'm the man so that's my job.' (Rick, father of two who works part-time and his wife works full-time)

Such parental gender stereotyping has been previously observed in a US context to have a detrimental effect on both mothers and fathers in the workplace (Correll & Ridgeway, 2006; Correll et al., 2007; Berdahl & Moon, 2013), and the data from the theme of 'Think Child–Think Mum' can be observed to support these findings in a UK context.

Due to the prevalence of 'Think Child–Think Mum', wider exploration is necessary and sub-themes are employed in an attempt to more fully explain why the caregiving father, depicted as a part-time father applicant in the online vignette survey (Chap. 2), obtained lower ratings than the other working parent scenarios. Thus, the overarching theme of 'Think Child–Think Mum' also contains two sub-themes entitled "Where's Mum?" and 'Unconventionality'.

"Where Is Mum?"

The sub-theme of "Where is Mum?" appeared frequently in both working parent and manager interviews. The phrase can be seen as an enactment of 'Think Child–Think Mum', in circumstances when the assumed primary association between mothers and caregiving is challenged by caregiving fathers. Such fathers can expect probes regarding the presence of fathers and the absence of mothers. In the working parent interviews fathers who took an active role in caregiving unanimously gave examples of "Where is Mum", as Paul, a single father of one and who works part-time, explained:

> If he (my son) had a hospital appointment, it would be like, well, why is the Dad going to the hospital with them?

Paul continued that whilst a request for absence due to caregiving would normally be granted, the whereabouts of his son's mother would be questioned by his manager:

> I suppose if you have to go, you're going to need to go, "what about his mother?" that was quite often the question I was asked.

It is important to note that whilst such requests for information appear quite innocuous and not necessarily intended to indicate disapproval, some caregiving fathers considered such comments to be more significant. Jack, a father of two who worked on a part-time basis when his children were younger, and is married to a full-time working mother, stated:

> I was often asked 'Where's Jacob's mother?' things like that. And although they weren't barbed in any way, I could tell that they were kind of meant to be … although they were just supposedly innocent questions, I think that there was a bit more of a point to them.

Corey, a full-time working father of three in a family where both he and his wife worked full-time, also experienced 'Where is Mum?' remarks:

> It isn't necessarily a big deal, but whenever I go anywhere for the kids, plays, school pick-ups that sort of thing, the first thing I am asked is '(mum) couldn't make it?' I am sure they are just making conversation, but I find it rude, and I don't know what to say really.

From these comments, it appears that such remarks made within the workplace and in a more general social context may have a negative impact on fathers which could potentially create a barrier to fathers undertaking caregiving responsibilities.

It is important to note that the reverse phenomena of "Where is Dad?" did not emerge in interviews with mothers, and can be considered as conspicuous by its absence, indicating that the association of caregiving and mothers is presumed, and thus the location of the father was not relevant.

The notion of "Where is Mum?" also emerged in the manager interviews. Jon, an HR manager in a military organisation, commented that in their organisation, they have some fathers who work part-time; however, questions are raised about the location of the mother. He stated:

> This is where you see that sort of stereotype you know, where's the mother? Why are you doing it?

Similarly, Lois, a hospital manager, stated that when fathers want to work part-time, the question often asked is, "Why would you (work part-time) because you've got a wife". This was further endorsed by Laura, a line manager, who stated, "I still think the response in a lot of the workplaces would be: 'Well, why can't your wife do that?'"

The examples above denote illustrations of the differences in how men and women perceive their role as caregiver and how such a role is perceived by others. However, one specific way in which caregiving fathers were judged was more prominent and therefore has been established as an additional sub-theme, and this focuses around judgements of 'Unconventionality'.

Unconventionality

As proposed earlier in this chapter, according to the gender stereotyping literature, parents who move away from behavioural norms can expect to face sanctions (Chesley, 2011). The sub-theme of 'Unconventionality' within the 'Fatherhood Forfeit Study' explores statements made by participants alluding to caregiving fathers as being somewhat different from the 'norm'. In interviews with working parents, it was widely apparent that parents who challenged gender norms, typically regarding the extent of involvement in caregiving responsibilities, often felt that others perceived their choice to be 'unconventional'. Paul, a single father of one who worked part-time, explained that when he told people about his working hours, the standard response was, "Oh, that's a bit weird, that's a bit odd". Similarly, Jack, who worked part-time whilst his wife worked full-time when his children we young stated:

> When our eldest son was very young ... she [his wife] was the person that made most of the money, and she was sort of the main breadwinner ... I had to spend a couple of days a week as the kind of stay-at-home parent ... I think that that was ... seen as a sort of unusual thing ... it was just less normal to see a male parent providing most of the childcare to a young baby ... I think it was something that although not really sneered at and not, like I say, frowned upon, it was probably something that wasn't considered to be quite normal.

It is plausible that such perceptions of 'Unconventionality', as intimated above, might have an impact on the extent of paternal involvement in caregiving and explain the adherence to the breadwinner model for many UK fathers. The concept of caregiving fathers being viewed as unconventional was described by some participants as originating from childhood experiences which is consistent with existing literature in this area (Croft et al., 2014; Levtov et al., 2015). This is illustrated by the experience of Kelly, a full-time working mother of one and whose partner worked on a part-time basis. She felt her more traditional, breadwinning brothers were critical of the working arrangements of her family. She noted that "their wives have stayed at home, they have provided everything, but that's what they want, that's what they have come from, that is what my mum did".

Such notions of parental behavioural norms originating from personal childhood experiences of traditional gendered divisions of parenting responsibilities also regularly emerged in the data. This was evidenced by Terry, Caitlin and Amy:

> I think it is something we've talked about (both our fathers working full-time and mothers working part-time) and are aware it is something new to us, alien, we hadn't experienced it so were a kind of a bit cautious, quite a bit … we thought 'this is different to what we know'. (Terry, a father of two who took extended SPL and whose wife works full-time)

> My husband has never felt comfortable with me working (and him not) … I think that is because of what he always knew with his Mum. His mum was always at home, so that is what he thought mums and dads should do. (Caitlin, a mother of two who works full-time and whose husband was a stay-at-home dad)

> My mum stayed at home, my dad went out to work you know so that's the way I've been brought up so no, I think I probably wouldn't have it (a father working part-time). (Amy, a team leader)

Such feelings of being unconventional were also demonstrated as coming from peers, as expressed by Caitlin, a mother of two, who works full-time and was married to a stay-at-home dad:

> He didn't mix with many other fathers … He didn't see them at the school gate (they were at work). … I suppose men at the school gate are a bit strange.

This was echoed by Sid, a father of four, who combined primary care-giving with self-employment and whose wife works full-time:

> Generally the response (when I say I am a stay at home dad) is one of surprise. I feel like I am encroaching on someone else's territory. On passport forms, the mothers name come first … this is just another one of the things … when I say I am the main one at home for the kids, people will quickly move over the subject, it is such an unusual thing for people to understand … I see the mums bring kids to schools; they are fabulous and very committed, it is natural … I suppose I feel a fraud at times … I have felt it quite profoundly.

Such judgements can be conceptualised as potentially having an implication on the extent of involvement of fathers in caregiving and offer partial explanations for the maintenance of the status quo in which mothers are the primary caregivers and fathers are aligned to breadwinning.

Emma, a mother of two who works full-time whilst her partner works part-time, observed that whilst colleagues did not seem to be judgemental about her decision to work full-time, she felt that her choice was viewed as diverging from accepted standards; she stated:

> When I had my first son, I had to go back to work full-time and, yeah, that certainly raised some eyebrows. I think it wasn't considered to be particularly the norm … I think it was far less likely that a mother would go back to work until the children were at school, part-time and certainly not full-time … people seemed a little bit sort of concerned by it … they were expecting me to be away from work for longer certainly.

Similarly, Liv, a mother of one, felt that her manager assumed she would want to work part-time after the birth of her son: "I kind of had an informal chat with the founder … he said look, I know you'll be wanting to come back part-time".

The data are suggestive that parents who challenge gender norms face perceptions of 'Unconventionality' from numerous directions including colleagues, extended family, peers and within their own families. It is proposed that within this climate, maintenance of the status quo might become a driving force for parental decision-making regarding caregiving and working arrangements.

It is relevant to note that perceptions of 'Unconventionality' were not limited to interviews with working parents and also emerged regularly in interviews with managers. Manager interviews provided further evidence that caregiving fathers are conceptualised as deviating from the traditional assumptions of paternal behaviour and are associated with being unconventional as demonstrated by Helen, Sam and Clare:

> The challenges for fathers are a lot less spoken about, so we do have some fathers who have taken paternity leave, and that in itself is quite rare … he has taken a lot more sick days since he became a parent. We don't treat him any differently, but it stands out more because he is a male, and he is caring for children which is against the norm almost, it is just assumed that the man will go to work and the woman will stay at home. (Helen, a manager at a recruitment agency)

We allow women to go off and look after their kids but perhaps not men so much, and they might feel that. That actually, it is more difficult for them because they are seen, as you know, I am staying here; I am the worker, so they have to stay in work and perhaps … I suspect they probably feel that they do have to stay in work, and they can't go off, and perhaps they might be looked on differently. (Sam, a ward manager)

I think it would be quite … it would be unusual … we haven't had any … Oh, the discussion would be very interesting … I think it would just throw them if it was a man working part-time because we don't have any men working part-time … a bit kind of 'oh dunno!' (Clare, an HR manager at a technology company)

CHAPTER SUMMARY

This chapter began by charting the existing literature surrounding the issues of gender stereotyping in a general sense, specific parental gender stereotyping and how this impacts upon the workplace experiences for parents. It explored how workplace behaviour is often guided by prescriptive gender bias through a complex matrix of sanctions and rewards based on alignment to expected norms of parental behaviour which often originate from childhood and are evidenced to continue via occupational sex typing. Data from the qualitative element of the 'Fatherhood Forfeit Study' was presented, and through the theme of 'Think Mum-Think Child', it was identified that mothers are regularly automatically associated with children and established as primary caregivers regardless of individual family arrangements which impact upon the workplace experiences and perceptions of caregiving fathers.

It was proposed that caregiving fathers are often faced with "Where is Mum?" questions when attempting to navigate between caregiving and work, further emphasising their secondary positioning. Additionally, it was highlighted that fathers who deviate from traditional breadwinning patterns of working hours face judgements of 'Unconventionality'.

Although causality is not explored in the 'Fatherhood Forfeit Study', potentially one of the impacts of the data encapsulated within the theme 'Think- Child–Think Mum' is the data presented within the following chapter which explores the second theme of the qualitative data: 'Fathers obtain less workplace support than mothers for caregiving'.

References

Anderson, V. (2009). *Research methods in human resource management* (2nd ed.). Chartered Institute of Personnel Development.

Atwater, L. E., & Van Fleet, D. D. (1997). Another ceiling? Can males compete for traditionally female jobs? *Journal of Management, 23*(5), 603–626. Available at: http://journals.sagepub.com. Accessed 28 Sept 2018.

Barnett, R. C., & Hyde, J. S. (2001). Women, men, work and family: An expansionist theory. *American Psychologist, 56*(10), 781–796. https://doi.org/1 0.1037/0003-066X.56.10.781

Baxter, J. (2010). *The language of female leadership.* Palgrave Macmillan.

Beaulieu, M.D., Hudon, É, Roberge, D., Pineault, R., Forte, D. and Legare, J. (1999) 'Practice guidelines for clinical prevention: Do patients, physicians and experts share common ground?', Canadian Medical Association, 161(5), pp. 519-523. Available at: http://www.cmaj.ca/content/161/5/519.

Beloff, H. (1992). Mother, father and me: Our IQ. *The Psychologist, 5,* 309–311.

Berdahl, J. L., & Moon, S. H. (2013). Workplace mistreatment of middle class workers based on sex, parenthood and caregiving. *Journal of Social Issues, 69*(2), 341–366. https://doi.org/10.1111/josi.12018

Berryman-Fink, C., Ballard-Reisch, D. & Newman, L. H. (eds). (2015). *Communication and sex-role socialization.* New York: Routledge.

Biernat, M. (1991). Gender stereotypes and the relationship between masculinity and femininity: A developmental analysis. *Journal of Personality and Social Psychology, 61*(3), 351–365. https://doi.org/10.1037/0022-3514.61.3.351

Braun, V. & Clarke, V. (2006). Using thematic analysis in psychology. *Qualitative research in psychology, 3*(2), pp. 77–101.

Broadbridge, A., & Hearn, J. (2008). Gender and management: New directions in research and continuing patterns in practice. *British Journal of Management, 19*(s1), S38–S49. https://doi.org/10.1111/j.1467-8551.2008.00570.x

Carr-Ruffino, N. (1993). *The promotable woman.* Van Nostrand.

Carter, D. C. (1987). *Current conceptions of sex roles and sex typing: Theory and research.* Praeger.

Charmaz, in Denzin, N. K., & Lincoln, Y. S. (2005). *The Sage handbook of qualitative research.* Sage.

Chesley, N. (2011). Stay-at-home fathers and breadwinning mothers: Gender, couple dynamics, and social change. *Gender & Society, 25*(5), 642–664.

Collinson, D. L. (1988). Engineering humour': Masculinity, joking and conflict in shop-floor relations. *Organization Studies, 9*(2), 181–199.

Collinson, D. L., Knights, D., & Collinson, M. (1990). *Managing to discriminate.* Routledge.

Correll, S. J., & Ridgeway, C. L. (2006). Expectation states theory. In *Handbook of social psychology* (pp. 29–51). Springer.

Correll, S., Benard, S., & Paik, I. (2007). Getting a job: Is there a motherhood penalty? *American Journal of Sociology, 112*(5), 1297–1338.

Croft, A., Schmader, T., Block, K., & Baron, A. S. (2014). The second shift reflected in the second generation: Do parents' gender roles at home predict children's aspirations? *Psychological Science, 25*(7), 1418–1428. https://doi.org/10.1177/0956797614533968

Cunningham, M. (2001). The influence of parental attitudes and behaviors on children's attitudes toward gender and household labor in early adulthood. *Journal of Marriage and Family, 63*(1), 111–122.

Denzin, N. K. & Lincoln, Y. S. (eds). (2017). *The Sage handbook of qualitative research.* 5th edn; Sage Publications.

Eagly, A. H. (1987). *Sex differences in social behaviour – A social role interpretation.* Lawrence Erlbaum Associates.

Eagly, A. H., & Karau, S. J. (2002). Role congruity theory of prejudice toward female leaders. *Psychological Review, 109*(3), 573–598.

Eagly, A. H., & Koenig, A. M. (2008). Gender prejudice: On the risks of occupying incongruent roles. In *Beyond common sense: Psychological science in the courtroom* (pp. 63–81). Blackwell Publishing Ltd. https://doi.org/10.1002/9780470696422.ch4

Eagly, A. H., & Mladinic, A. (1989). Gender stereotypes and attitudes toward women and men. *Personality and Social Psychology Bulletin, 15*(4), 543–558.

Eccles, J. S. (1983). 'Expectancies, values, and academic behaviors', in Spence, J. T. (ed.), *Achievement and achievement motivation.* San Francisco: W. H. Freeman, pp. 75–146.

Eccles, J. S., Jacobs, J. E., & Harold, R. D. (1990). Gender role stereotypes, expectancy effects, and parents' socialization of gender differences. *Journal of Social Issues, 46*(2), 183–201.

Erikson, E. H. (1968). Life cycle. In *International encyclopaedia of the social sciences* (Vol. 9, pp. 286–292).

Flynn, F. J., & Ames, D. R. (2006). What's good for the goose may not be as good for the gander: The benefits of self-monitoring for men and women in task groups and dyadic conflicts. *Journal of Applied Psychology, 91*(2), 272–281.

Freud, S. (1953). Three essays on the theory of sexuality (1905). In *The standard edition of the complete psychological works of Sigmund Freud, Volume VII (1901–1905): A case of hysteria, three essays on sexuality and other works* (pp. 123–246).

Gerson, K. (1993). *No man's land: Men's changing commitments to family and work.* Basic Books.

Giddens, A., & Sutton, P. W. (2013). *Sociology.* Indian Reprint.

Glick, P., Zion, C., & Nelson, C. (1988). What mediates sex discrimination in hiring decisions? *Journal of Personality and Social Psychology, 55*(2), 178–186.

Hammersley, M., & Atkinson, P. (2007). *Ethnography: Principles in practice*. Routledge.

Harkness, S., & Super, C. M. (1995). Culture and parenting. In M. Bornstein (Ed.), *Handbook of parenting* (Biology and ecology of parenting) (Vol. 2, pp. 211–234). Lawrence Erlbaum Associates.

Heilman, M. E. (2001). 'Description and prescription: How gender stereotypes prevent women's ascent up the organizational ladder', *Journal of Social Issues, 57*(4), pp. 657–674.

Heilman, M. E., & Parks-Stamm, E. J. (2007). Gender stereotypes in the workplace: Obstacles to women's career progress. In S. J. Correll (Ed.), *Social psychology of gender* (Advances in group processes, 24) (pp. 47–77). Emerald Group Publishing Limited.

Heilman, M. E., & Wallen, A. S. (2010). Wimpy and undeserving of respect: Penalties for men's gender-inconsistent success. *Journal of Experimental Social Psychology, 46*(4), 664–667.

Hofferth, S. L. (1999). 'Child care, maternal employment, and public policy', *The Annals of the American Academy of Political and Social Science, 563*(1), pp. 20–38.

Holmes, J. (2006). Sharing a laugh: Pragmatic aspects of humor and gender in the workplace. *Journal of Pragmatics, 38*(1), 26–50.

Howell, K. E. (2013). *The philosophy of methodology*. Sage.

Kaplan, S. J. (1991). 'Katherine Mansfield and the origins of modernist fiction', In Greene, A. M. and Kirton, G. (2015), The dynamics of managing diversity: A critical approach. Routledge.

Kelan, E. K. (2010). Gender logic and (un) doing gender at work. *Gender, Work and Organization, 17*(2), 174–194.

Ku, C. M. (2011). When does gender matter? Gender differences in speciality choice among physicians. *Work and Occupations, 38*(2), 221–262.

Langford, T., & MacKinnon, N. J. (2000). The affective bases for the gendering of traits: Comparing the United States and Canada. *Social Psychology Quarterly, 63*(1), 34–48.

Leidner, R. (1993). *Fast food, fast talk: Service work and the routinization of everyday life*. University of California Press.

Levtov, R., Van Der Gaag, N., Greene, M., Kaufman, M., & Barker, G. (2015). *State of the world's fathers: A MenCare advocacy publication*. Promundo, Rutgers, Save the Children, Sonke Gender Justice, and the MenEngage Alliance. Available at: https://www.savethechildren.net/sites/default/files/libraries/state-of-the-worlds-fathers_12-june-2015.pdf.   Accessed   28 Sept 2018.

Lincoln, Y. S., & Guba, E. G. (1985). *Naturalistic inquiry* (Vol. 75). Sage.

Lobel, M. (1994). 'Conceptualizations, measurement, and effects of prenatal maternal stress on birth outcomes', *Journal of Behavioral Medicine, 17*(3), pp. 225–272.

Lobel, T. E., Gruber, R., Govrin, N., & Mashraki-Pedhatzur, S. (2001). Children's gender-related inferences and judgments: A cross-cultural study. *Developmental Psychology, 37*(6), 839.

Luzadis, R., Wesolowski, M., & Snavely, B. (2008). Understanding criterion choice in hiring decisions from a prescriptive gender bias perspective. *Journal of Managerial Issues, 20*(4), 468–484.

Marks, J. L., Lam, C. B., & McHale, S. M. (2009). Family patterns of gender role attitudes. *Sex Roles, 61,* 221–234. https://doi.org/10.1007/s11199-009-9619-3. Available at: https://www.ncbi.nlm.nih.gov/pmc/articles/PMC3270818/. Accessed 28 Sept 2018.

Miles, M. B., & Huberman, A. M. (1994). *Qualitative data analysis: An expanded sourcebook.* Sage.

Mischel, W. (1966). The social learning view of sex differences in behaviour. In E. E. Maccoby (Ed.), *The development of sex differences.* Stanford University Press.

Moss-Racusin, C. A., Dovidio, J. F., Brescoll, V. L., Graham, M. J., & Handelsman, J. (2012). Science faculty's subtle gender biases favor male students. *Proceedings of the National Academy of Sciences, 109*(41), 16474–16479.

Nadler, J. T., & Stockdale, M. S. (2012). Workplace gender bias: Not between just strangers. *North American Journal of Psychology, 14*(2), 281–292.

Noon, M. (2012). Simply the best? The case for using 'threshold selection' in hiring decisions. *Human Resource Management Journal, 22*(1), 76–88.

Padavic, I., & Reskin, B. F. (2002). *Women and men at work.* Pine Forge Press.

Pleck, E. H., & Pleck, J. H. (1997). Fatherhood ideals in the United States: Historical dimensions. In M. E. Lamb (Ed.), *The role of the father in child development* (3rd ed., pp. 33–48). Wiley.

Rudman, L. A. & Phelan, J. E. (2008). 'Backlash effects for disconfirming gender stereotypes in organizations', *Research in Organizational Behavior, 28,* pp. 61–79. https://doi.org/10.1016/j.riob.2008.04.003

Santrock, J. (1994). *Child development* (6th ed.). Brown & Benchmark.

Sheppard, M. (2004). *Appraising and using social research in the human sciences.* Jessica Kingsley Publishers.

Sheridan, A. (2004). Chronic presenteeism: The multiple dimensions to men's absence from part time work. *Gender, Work and Organization, 11*(2), 207–225.

Silverman, D. (2000). *Doing qualitative research: A practical handbook.* Sage.

Silverstein, M., Conroy, S. J., Wang, H., Giarrusso, R. and Bengtson, V. L., (2002). 'Reciprocity in parent-child relations over the adult life course', *The Journals of Gerontology Series B: Psychological Sciences and Social Sciences, 57*(1), pp. S3–S13.

Sinno, S. M., & Killen, M. (2009). Moms at work and dads at home: Children's evaluations of parental roles. *Applied Developmental Science, 13*(1), 16–29. https://doi.org/10.1080/10888690802606735

Thorne, B. (1993). *Gender play.* Rutgers University Press.

Whittaker, A. (2009). *Research skills for social work*. Learning Matters Ltd.
Witt, S. D. (2000). The influence of peers on children's socialization to gender roles. *Early Child Development and Care, 162*(1), 1–7.
Wood, W., & Eagly, A. H. (2002). A cross-cultural analysis of the behavior of women and men: Implications for the origins of sex differences. *Psychological Bulletin, 128*(5), 699–727. https://doi.org/10.1037/0033-2909.128.5.699

Fathers Obtain Less Workplace Support Than Mothers for Caregiving

Abstract This chapter explores the notion that caregiving fathers in the workplace receive less support than their female counterparts. It begins by charting the current knowledge which identifies the ways in which organisations provide workplace support for parents with emphasis on the experiences of fathers. In particular, it explores literature which outlines workplace outcomes when fathers challenge the purported social norms by seeking more flexible working patterns to enable an active role in the caregiving of their children.

The data obtained within the qualitative element of the 'Fatherhood Forfeit Study' are focused upon within this chapter and illustrative quotes from study participants are employed to explore the workplace perceptions and experiences of caregiving fathers. Emphasis is placed upon data grouped under the overarching theme of 'Fathers obtain less workplace support than mothers for caregiving'. Due to the vast amount of data collected within this theme, a sub-theme has been created entitled 'Support is conditional and subject to negotiation for fathers' which specifically explores the contingent nature of workplace support for fathers which is suggested to be more negotiable than the support offered to mothers.

Keywords Fathers • Workplace Support • Childcare • Flexible working • Parents

© The Author(s), under exclusive license to Springer Nature Switzerland AG 2022
J. Kelland, *Caregiving Fathers in the Workplace*,
https://doi.org/10.1007/978-3-030-97971-3_4

WORKPLACE SUPPORT FOR PARENTS

As explored in Chap. 2, the contribution of fathers to caregiving has increased over time as observed both within academic literature and within the 'grey literature' through reports produced by bodies such as the Trade Union Congress, ACAS and Women and Equalities Select Committee. Contemporary fathers are suggested to navigate both work and home spheres through accessing gender neutral working policies and practices such as flexible working and part-time working, with increasing number of fathers accessing such working arrangements (Burnett et al., 2013; Working Families, 2019). However, labour market statistics are consistent in illustrating that fathers continue to dominate the realms of full-time employment with only 4.8% of fathers reducing hours due to childcare compared to 28.5% of mothers (ONS, 2019). Such an observation implies that any revolution towards gender equality is further away than may appear on the surface and a gap has been observed between a father's desire to be actively involved in caregiving and organisational support for this behaviour (Miller, 2010; Esping-Andersen et al., 2013). Workplace support for fathers as parents has been found by many academics to be limited (Crompton, 2002; Smithson & Stokoe, 2005; Tracy & Rivera, 2010) with fathers at work being observed to face 'invisibility' in their role as a father, being described as a "ghost in the organisational machine" (Burnett et al., 2013: 21).

Fathers have been observed to face a number of specific challenges when accessing policies that will assist them with managing the dual demands of work and caregiving (Smithson et al., 2004; Lewis et al., 2007). The existing literature that explores the challenges facing fathers in accessing organisational support has been identified as having three main strands which centre around the lack of awareness of workplace policies for fathers, fathers being less likely to request organisational support and also being less likely to receive support if they do request it.

Firstly, fathers have been found to have a lack of awareness regarding the different types of policies available to them to assist with caregiving (Sheridan, 2004; Kersley et al., 2006; Mercer, 2017). Such a lack of awareness has also been observed on the part of employers, with Cook et al. (2020) observing that employers are often unaware of the applicability of such policies to fathers. Secondly, fathers have been observed to be less likely to ask for flexibility in working arrangements than mothers (Teasdale, 2012), with some fathers reporting a fear of asking for greater flexibility and thus concealing any work-life conflict (Mercer, 2017). This perhaps isn't surprising in light of research which has found that fathers who work less than full time hours are rated as less professionally competent than those who work full-time (Brescoll & Uhlmann, 2005; Berdahl & Moon, 2013). A further explanation for why men might be less likely to request amendments to working arrangements due to caregiving is suggested to be due to men having a lower sense of entitlement than women with regard to access to such working arrangements (Lewis & Smithson, 2001; Gatrell et al., 2014; Cook et al., 2020). Thirdly, fathers have been found to be more likely to face rejection than mothers when requesting an amended working pattern, whether informal or formal, due to caregiving reasons (Fagan et al., 2006; Holter, 2007; Dex et al., 2008; Tracy & Rivera, 2010; Munsch, 2016). For many, workplace support for caregiving is a consequence of a period of negotiation, and this has been found to be specifically prevalent for fathers, and in this negotiation, fathers have been suggested to have less power than mothers (Brandth & Kvande, 2002; Bloksgaard, 2014). Furthermore, the 'flexibility stigma', which is a key barrier to many in the uptake of flexible working, is reported more commonly by men, specifically fathers, who are less likely to reduce their working hours or believe that this is an option for them (Vandello et al., 2008; Williams et al., 2013; Chung, 2018; Cook et al., 2020). Thus, workplace support for caregiving behaviour can be conceptualised as a potential favour, a maternal privilege which is often not afforded to fathers (Lewis, 1997; Atkinson & Hall, 2009; Gatrell & Cooper, 2016).

In the light of the challenges for fathers surrounding workplace support for caregiving behaviours, perhaps it is unsurprising that for many families, more traditional divisions of parental roles and associated patterns of work might prevail, and this will be explored in detail through the data obtained within the qualitative element of the 'Fatherhood Forfeit Study'.

FATHERHOOD FORFEIT STUDY DATA

The quantitative element of the 'Fatherhood Forfeit Study' as presented in Chap. 2 specifically addressed the flexible working practice of part-time working which was presented as a mechanism by which parents can enable active involvement in family life. It was observed that the caregiving father (represented as an applicant for a part-time role) obtained the lowest score out of all four of the working parent scenarios, which is indicative that caregiving fathers face disparity in the workplace and are less likely to obtain working arrangements that are conducive to caregiving. The qualitative data collected through semi-structured interviews with working parents and managers and vignette-based manager focus groups sought to obtain potential explanations for this and an overarching theme that emerged was the theme that 'Fathers obtain less workplace support than mothers for caregiving'.

'Fathers Obtain Less Workplace Support than Mothers for Caregiving'

This overarching theme was a recurrent theme in interviews with managers, as illustrated by these quotes from manager participants:

> It is viewed differently [requests from fathers for flexibility] and maybe not looked at as empathetically … in the same way as if it was a female. (Samantha, HR manager)

> He (a father) would be looked at differently than a mum … I think that sometimes it is easier perhaps for people to think of the mum taking time off with maternity leave and all that than the dad, and they would be more supportive, intentionally or not … if the child is sick … it tends to affect the women more than the men, in fact, I can't really think of a time when I have seen any of my male colleagues have to stay home. (Sophie, line manager, NHS)

> There are policies for working mothers and a whole range of agreements arranged locally … we accommodate it for maternal parents; we let them park nearby, simple things like that, however, when it comes to fathers we could do more. (Jon, HR manager in a military organisation)

> We probably are more flexible with them [mothers] I imagine than we would be with men. (Sam, line manager)

Clare, an HR manager, presented a slightly more positive viewpoint and stated, "I think we would treat a mother who works part-time the same as a father". However, she believes the management response to fathers would differ from that to mothers; in particular, she believes that for a mother, managers would "worry more about providing flexibility", than they would for a father, implying that it might be more challenging for fathers to work flexibly as this is not expected to be required in the same way that it is for mothers.

The interviews with working parents provided further insights regarding disparities in the workplace support afforded to caregiving fathers, with numerous comments made regarding a reduced level of support for caregiving fathers:

> Comparing it (the level of support) with a colleague who was a female, I would say I had slightly less support. (Paul, a single father of one who works part-time)

> Informally, there is that sort of support network there, that sort of invisible support network amongst mothers that just kind of know what it is like to have to juggle an awful lot. (Emma, works full-time, is married and has two children and whose husband works part-time)

Sue, also a full-time working mother of two whose husband works part-time, believes that the challenges in requesting alternative work patterns are both actual and perceived. She stated:

> Women probably are in a better position ... in terms of culture and how people accept that. For fathers there is a different pressure from a personal perspective around requesting that time. As to how that would be viewed, so whether that's because of what's happened or whether it's believed there's an internal conflict around doing that, around how they feel that that's viewed and whether that's lived out or not is different because sometimes people don't ask because they have a belief.

Such a viewpoint aligns closely to existing literature which is suggestive that caregiving fathers might obtain less workplace support due to an incumbent belief amongst them that they would be less likely to obtain it and subsequently they do not request alternative patterns of working, thus creating a self-fulfilling prophecy (Sheridan, 2004; Allard et al., 2011; Gatrell & Cooper, 2016). Certainly, the results of the quantitative element of this study, as discussed in Chap. 2, point to this being a reality rather than an inaccurate presumption.

Examples of workplace flexibility to support the management of dual spheres were lacking in the interviews with working fathers within the 'Fatherhood Forfeit Study' which is quite conspicuous in its absence. In contrast, it was proposed by David, a father of three who works full-time, that within his job he has "no real flexibility, if it was more flexible that would be good".

By way of comparison, the qualitative data from the 'Fatherhood Forfeit Study' was consistent in demonstrating that mothers in the workplace appeared to receive wider support for caregiving, with many participants giving examples of how mothers are supported in the workplace and sharing their ideas of how mothers might be supported further with mechanisms varying from preferential parking to altered work patterns. Working mothers themselves also seemed to endorse the existence of informal workplace flexibility for their role as a parent:

> If I've got the little one's Christmas play that I need two or three hours [away from work] that I know that I've got two or three hours that I can take, and nobody's going to question me on that. (Stephanie, a married mother of two, both she and her husband work flexibly)

> [I have] always had supportive colleagues, who have never made me feel guilty if I have had to take any time off because the children were sick. (Lyn, a mother of two in a family in which both parents work full-time)

The data within the overarching theme of 'Fathers obtain less workplace support than mothers for caregiving' are consistent with existing academic knowledge as outlined earlier in this chapter (Lewis et al., 2007). Specifically, the data from the 'Fatherhood Forfeit Study' support assertions that fathers and managers lack awareness of the applicability of workplace arrangements that support caregiving of fathers (Cook et al., 2020). The findings of this study also support existing research which found that fathers are less likely than mothers to ask for such arrangements, either formally or informally and are less likely to obtain them (Teasdale, 2012; Munsch, 2016). The data within this overarching theme also offer direct explanations for the results of the online vignette in which the part-time father applicant received the lowest ratings of all applicants.

Due to the amount of data within this overarching theme, further classification was needed, and a sub-theme was identified. The discussion now turns to explore the sub-theme that 'Support is conditional and subject to negotiation for Fathers'. This sub-theme explores the circumstances in which a father takes on caregiving responsibilities, and the extent of negotiation embarked upon with the employer or potential employer and appears to directly impact upon the likelihood of workplace support being obtained. Such elements of conditionality and negotiation emerged only in relation to discussion with, or about, fathers and did not emerge for working mothers and is thus worthy of deeper exploration.

'Support Is Conditional and Subject to Negotiation for Fathers'

It was apparent in both manager and working parent interviews that support for caregiving fathers was both conditional and subject to negotiation, with any provision being contingent on circumstances. Whilst direct comparisons between mothers and fathers experiences were not a focus of this study, it was observable that conditionality and negotiation did not emerge to the same extent within discussions about mothers or from mother participants. In over half of the manager interviews, respondents referred to fathers negotiating with line managers when they needed to take unexpected leave for caregiving, whereas for mothers such negotiations were not mentioned. For example, Amy, a team leader, stated:

(Fathers are) almost waiting to be given permission ... I get the feeling that (for mothers) it's not a negotiation, it's just "we've got to go"; (fathers) don't expect to be let off as easily ... it's almost assumed by the women that that's what happens, you know? They have to go straight away, whereas I think the men I work with seem to make more of a story about it.

In the interviews, working parents (predominantly fathers) widely demonstrated the centrality of negotiation for fathers in the workplace. Paul, a single father of one and who worked part-time, outlined the process in more detail:

(For mothers) it was almost like, we don't want to know the reasons why you need to be off, but you can have the time off ... it is almost like we don't want to know too much because you're the mother. Whereas if I went ... they weren't so forgiving in terms of always giving me time off. Sometimes it was quite a battle to try to get that time off ... I would say, well, you know, I'll see if my Mum's free ... but primarily it was me wanting to go and to pick him up and to make sure he was okay and you know, after a few questions, they would then let me go... the first question I would get is, 'is there nobody else that can have him, could I ring family, could I ring friends'.

Paul continued to narrate an example of when he attempted to make adjustments to his working pattern to enable him to continue to pick up his son from school:

There was an instance when my contract was being adjusted and it was suggested I make myself more available than I had been. As my contract gave me Tuesdays off, I was regularly doing the school run. However, the new management wanted me to work half a day with no exception. At first, I was concerned that my only day to do the school run would be affected. That being said, I did make an offer that I do my shift after the school run, and before the school pick up. They did agree - eventually, but only after I had to fully justify it, I don't think they would have done that to a mother, I think I would have had more support.

For working fathers, the words "negotiation", "battle", "justification" and "making a fuss" all emerged from the data as part of the process of attempting to obtain workplace support. Such comments were largely absent in the discussion with, or about, working mothers. For example, fathers stated:

[if a child is sick] I can normally go .... But [my manager] will always make such a fuss it is normally easier if my wife gets them. (Corey, a father of three in a family in which both parents work full-time)

If Nicola was in the middle of shift ... I'd probably come home ... I'd negotiate it ... there are some people who on agreement they leave early ... should their spouse not be able to pick them up and they have agreed, they'll talk to their manager. (David, a full-time working father of three whose wife works part-time)

This example illustrates that the experiences of some fathers is that support can be obtained, but it requires negotiation, and in the latter case is contingent on the absence of the mother with agreement dependent on establishing her location and unavailability. These findings not only support existing research which observed an element of inherent negotiation for caregiving fathers (Brandth & Kvande, 2002; Bloksgaard, 2014), but has extended this further by identifying circumstances in which negotiation was more likely to be successful, namely, if the mother was absent. This was also apparent in the interviews with managers, where, once again, the amount of support for fathers appeared to be dictated by the location of the mother, and often this was quite covert. Sammi, a ward manager, explained that parental status would not be a factor for a father during the selection process unless "he was a single father and he'd said, 'I've got a young child' ". Such statements seem to imply that it is the absence of the mother that determines the level of support received by the father rather than fatherhood status in its own right. Similarly, Amy, a team leader, stated that "If my male colleague was a single parent, I'd probably be exactly the same [supportive]". She continued:

Amy: I think I probably wouldn't have it [give them support] unless they said they were a single parent or if they implied that their partner is ill or, you, know wasn't able to work or so ... but all that discussion would be in my head. It wouldn't be verbalised.
Interviewer: Yes. And why wouldn't it be verbalised?
Amy: Because I think you know we're not allowed to, are we? You know, but it would still be going on.

On some occasions, the scrutiny regarding family circumstances appeared to go deeper, with Jon, an HR manager in a military organisation, depicting a situation where a father requested to pick his child up from school a few days a week, and the decision to allow this involved the HR team considering, "Do they believe him? Is he credible? Is there a sharing order?" The implication being that if a legal arrangement didn't exist, and he was not deemed to be credible, workplace support would not be granted. Whilst Jon's account did not mention the differing reactions to mothers in the workplace, the previous data are indicative that a mother would be less likely to face such scrutiny.

This notion of conditionality builds upon existing theoretical understandings presented by Gatrell et al. (2014), who found that workplace flexibility was considered to be obtained by fathers only through competing with mothers. However, in the 'Fatherhood Forfeit Study' it is proposed that rather than obtaining support through competing with mothers it was obtained through demonstrating the lack of availability of the mother. This work informs academic debate by presenting new ways of understanding why caregiving fathers may obtain a reduced level of support, and the circumstances in which support can be obtained.

It is pertinent to note that the data in this theme are indicative of an issue beyond that of equality for parents, with caregiving fathers appearing to receive negative treatment in relation to caregiving behaviour rather than simply less favourable treatment, and this issue is returned to in Chap. 5 when discussing the 'Social Mistreatment of Caregiving Fathers'.

CHAPTER SUMMARY

The theme of 'Fathers obtain less workplace support than mothers for caregiving' was one of the most widely apparent and consistent themes in interviews with manager and working parent participants. The data were indicative that many support mechanisms exist in the workplace for parents, but that mothers are widely in receipt of them in a way that fathers are not. Whilst the types of support varied between participants, the reduced extent of the support was consistent. Empathy, understanding and access to working arrangements that facilitate caregiving, such as part-time and flexible working, were widely evident with regard to mothers, whereas for fathers this was not apparent.

The theme of 'Fathers obtain less workplace support than mothers for caregiving' and its sub-theme, 'Support is conditional and subject to negotiation for fathers', has shed further light on potential factors contributing to why the caregiving father depicted in the online vignette survey elements of the study obtained lower scores than their counterparts (as illustrated in Chap. 2). This chapter has offered various examples of the ways in which the differentials regarding workplace support for fathers exist. Such differentials are suggested here to have wide-ranging implications. In particular, if workplace support for mothers and fathers is not equalised, then the freedom of families to make their own choices on who (if anyone) is the primary caregiver will continue to be unfairly impacted by gender inequalities. The discussion will now move to the third and final theme that emerged from the qualitative data within the 'Fatherhood Forfeit Study' which explores the 'Social Mistreatment of Caregiving Fathers' and the potential impact this might have on continuation of gender inequalities in the workplace.

REFERENCES

Allard, K., Haas, L., & Hwang, C. P. (2011). Family-supportive organizational culture and fathers' experiences of work–family conflict in Sweden. *Gender, Work and Organization, 18*(2), 141–157. https://doi.org/10.1111/j.1468-0432.2010.00540.x

Atkinson, C. & Hall, L. (2009). 'The role of gender in varying forms of flexible working, *Gender, Work & Organization, 16*(6), pp. 650–666. https://doi.org/10.1111/j.1468-0432.2009.00456.x

Berdahl, J. L., & Moon, S. H. (2013). Workplace mistreatment of middle class workers based on sex, parenthood and caregiving. *Journal of Social Issues, 69*(2), 341–366. https://doi.org/10.1111/josi.12018

Bloksgaard, L. (2014). Negotiating leave in the workplace: Leave practices and masculinity constructions among Danish fathers. In *Fatherhood in the Nordic welfare states–comparing care policies and practice* (pp. 141–161).

Brandth, B., & Kvande, E. (2002). Reflexive fathers; negotiating parental leave and working life. *Gender, Work and Organization, 9*(2), 186–203. https://doi.org/10.1111/1468-0432.00155

Brescoll, V. L., & Uhlmann, E. L. (2005). Attitudes toward traditional and non-traditional parents. *Psychology of Women Quarterly, 29*(4), 436–445. Available at: http://www.socialjudgments.com/docs/Brescoll%20and%20Uhlmann%202005.pdf. Accessed 28 Sept 2018.

Burnett, S. B., Gatrell, C. J., Cooper, C. L., & Sparrow, P. (2013). Fathers at work: A ghost in the organizational machine. *Gender, Work and Organization, 20*(6), 632–646. https://doi.org/10.1111/gwao.12000

Chung, H. (2018). Gender, flexibility stigma and the perceived negative consequences of flexible working in the UK. *Social Indicators Research.* https://doi.org/10.1007/s11205-018-2036-7

Cook, R., O'Brien, M., Connolly, S., Aldrich, M., & Speight, S. (2020). Fathers' perceptions of the availability of flexible working arrangements: Evidence from the UK. *Work, Employment and Society,* 1–20. https://doi.org/10.1177/0950017020946687

Crompton, R. (2002). Employment, flexible working and the family. *British Journal of Sociology, 53*(4), 537–558.

Dex, S., Ward, K., & Joshi, H. (2008). Changes in women's occupations and occupational mobility over 25 years. In J. Scott, S. Dex, & H. Joshi (Eds.), *Women and employment: Changing lives and new challenges* (pp. 54–80). Edward Elgar. Available at: http://discovery.ucl.ac.uk/id/eprint/1490624. Accessed 28 Sept 2018.

Esping-Andersen, G., Boertien, D., Bonke, J., & Gracia, P. (2013). Couple specialisation in multiple equilibria. *European Sociological Review, 29*(6), 1280–1294.

Fagan, C., Hegewisch, A., & Pillinger, J. (2006). *Out of time: Why Britain needs a new approach to working-time flexibility.* Trade Union Congress.

Gatrell, C., & Cooper, C. L. (2016). A sense of entitlement? Fathers, mothers and organizational support for family and career. *Community, Work & Family, 19*(2), 134–147.

Gatrell, C. J., Burnett, S. B., Cooper, C. L., & Sparrow, P. (2014). Parents, perceptions and belonging: Exploring flexible working among UK fathers and mothers. *British Journal of Management, 25*(3), 473–487.

Holter, O. (2007). Men's work and family reconciliation in Europe. *Men and Masculinities, 9*(4), 425–456.

Kersley, B., Alpin, C., Forth, J., Bryson, A., Bewley, H., Dix, G., & Oxenbridge, S. (2006). *Inside the workplace: Findings from the 2004 workplace employment relations survey.* Routledge. Available at: http://cw.routledge.com/text-books/0415378133/about/resources.asp. Accessed 28 Sept 2021.

Lewis, S. (1997). Family friendly' policies: A route to changing organizations or playing around at the margins? *Gender, Work and Organization, 4*(1), 13–23. https://doi.org/10.1111/1468-0432.00020

Lewis, S., & Smithson, J. (2001). Sense of entitlement to support for the reconciliation of employment and family life. *Human Relations, 54*(11), 1455–1481.

Lewis, S., Gambles, R., & Rapoport, R. (2007). The constraints of a 'work–life balance' approach: An international perspective. *The International Journal of Human Resource Management, 18*(3), 360–373.

Mercer, M. (2017). *Flexible working for parents returning to work: Maintaining career development.* ACAS. Available at: https://www.employment-studies.co.uk/resource/flexible-working-parents-returning-work.   Accessed: 8 Nov 2021

Miller, T. (2010). *Making sense of fatherhood: Gender, caring and work.* Cambridge University Press.

Munsch, C. L. (2016). Flexible work, flexible penalties: The effect of gender, childcare, and type of request on the flexibility bias. *Social Forces, 94*(4), 1567–1591.

Office for National Statistics. (2019). Families in the labour market. Available at: https://www.ons.gov.uk/employmentandlabourmarket/peopleinwork/employmentandemployeetypes/articles/familiesandthelabourmarketengland/2019. Accessed 8 Nov 2021.

Sheridan, A. (2004). Chronic presenteeism: The multiple dimensions to men's absence from part time work. *Gender, Work and Organization, 11*(2), 207–225.

Smithson, J., Lewis, S., Cooper, C., & Dyer, J. (2004). Flexible working and the gender pay gap in the accountancy profession. *Work, Employment and Society, 18*(1), 115–135.

Smithson, J. & Stokoe, E. H. (2005). 'Discourses of work-life balance: Negotiating 'genderblind' terms in organizations', *Gender, Work & Organization, 12*(2), pp. 147–168.

Teasdale, N. (2012). Fragmented sisters? The implications of flexible working policies for professional women's workplace relationships. *Gender, Work and Organization, 20*(4), 349–346. https://doi.org/10.1111/j.1468-0432.2012.00590.x

Tracy, S. J., & Rivera, K. D. (2010). Endorsing equity and applauding stay-at-home moms: How male voices on work-life reveal aversive sexism and flickers of transformation. *Management Communication Quarterly, 24*(1), 3–43. https://doi.org/10.1177/0893318909352248

Vandello, J. A., Bosson, J. K., Cohen, D., Burnaford, R. M., & Weaver, J. R. (2008). Precarious manhood. *Journal of Personality and Social Psychology, 95*(6), 1325–1339. https://doi.org/10.1037/a0012453

Williams, J. C., Blair-Loy, M., & Berdahl, J. L. (2013). Cultural schemas, social class, and the flexibility stigma. *Journal of Social Issue, 69*(2), 209–234.

Working Families. (2019). *Modern families' index*. Available at: https://www.workingfamilies.org.uk/wp-content/uploads/2019/02/BH_MFI_Summary_Report_2019_Final.pdf. Accessed 4 Apr 2019.

CHAPTER 5

Social Mistreatment of Caregiving Fathers

Abstract This chapter presents existing knowledge regarding social and workplace outcomes when fathers challenge the purported gendered social norms through adjusting their working patterns to permit an active role in the caregiving of their children. Following this, the chapter offers further qualitative data obtained in the 'Fatherhood Forfeit Study', using illustrative quotes from semi-structured interviews and vignette-based manager focus groups to demonstrate the 'Social Mistreatment of Caregiving Fathers'.

This chapter focuses in detail on the most widely recurring themes of 'suspicion', 'mockery', 'struggling with friendships', 'negative judgement' and being 'viewed as idle'. As with previous chapters, the data from the 'Fatherhood Forfeit Study' will be linked to the existing academic terrain in this area, outlining the ways in which this work both corresponds with and contradicts existing knowledge.

Keywords Fathers • Suspicion • Mockery • Friendships • Negative Judgement • Being idle • Breadwinner/Breadwinning

J. Kelland, *Caregiving Fathers in the Workplace*, https://doi.org/10.1007/978-3-030-97971-3_5

SOCIAL AND WORKPLACE MISTREATMENT
OF CAREGIVING FATHERS

Much of the existing research in the area of parents at work focuses on the experience of mothers and identifies that working mothers face a varying number of penalties, such as perceptions of reduced commitment, impeded promotability and hireability (Fuegen et al., 2004; Ridgeway & Correll, 2004; Correll et al., 2007; Berdahl & Moon, 2013). The experience of fathers is often portrayed as the antithesis of this, aligned with workplace 'benefits' and 'premiums', such as being more likely to be promoted, having a higher starting salary and viewed as being more stable and committed than non-fathers and working mothers (Loh, 1996; Hersch & Stratton, 2000; Cuddy et al., 2004; Correll et al., 2007; Berdahl & Moon, 2013). Upon closer inspection, much of the research that has identified the emergence of 'benefits' for fathers and 'penalties' for mothers focuses on the comparison between mothers and fathers in full-time paid employment, in which fathers are arguably conforming to stereotypical breadwinning norms, whilst mothers who work full-time are contradicting the stereotypical norms. In this context, perhaps the pattern of 'penalties' and 'benefits' is not surprising. However, for caregiving fathers, research has found that the landscape alters, and they may experience workplace penalties akin to working mothers (Berdahl & Moon, 2013). This implies that employees of both genders face challenges when they behave in a way that is conceptualised as contrary to their gender, with such "gender deviants" facing significantly higher levels of workplace mistreatment than "gender conformers" (Berdahl et al., 1996; Gruber, 1998; Waldo et al., 1998; Berdahl, 2007: 346).

Academic discourse in the work and family arena points to a variety of challenges facing caregiving fathers, who can be conceptualised as moving away from traditional expectations of behaviour regarding fathering practices, implying that fathers might not be accepted at home in the same way that women are accepted arguably at the workplace (Pleck & Pleck, 1997; Lamb, 2004). For the purposes of this chapter, the challenges have been grouped under the theme of social mistreatment which was initially identified by Berdahl and Moon (2013) as a key mechanism for providing feedback and includes being teased, put down or excluded by colleagues. Such social mistreatment can be considered to be a central mechanism by which an immediate message regarding approval and status is transmitted (Duffy et al., 2006). This chapter explores the existing literature which identifies that caregiving fathers encounter mistreatment in the form of negative judgements, mockery, disapproval and discrimination, and social exclusion (Wayne & Cordeiro, 2003; Berdahl & Moon, 2013; Locke, 2016), all of which were also observable within the 'Fatherhood Forfeit Study'.

The 'Social Mistreatment of Caregiving Fathers' within both the workplace and in social settings has been observed by many academics to centre around issues of masculinity. Authors have suggested that caregiving fathers are conceptually stepping away from what is perceived to be acceptable behaviour for a 'real man' which is traditionally not associated with parenting and considered to be "not a fit occupation for men" (Podnieks, 2016; Connell, 1987: 106). Working fewer hours due to caregiving responsibilities may result in judgements of being less masculine and less worthy of respect then men who do not reduce work time in this way, with the actions of 'real men' being consistently linked to contribution to the household finances (Vandello et al., 2008; Rudman & Mescher, 2013; Burnett et al., 2013). Fathers who undertake a considerable amount of childcare have been observed to experience "not man enough" discrimination which centres around "being (judged as) insufficiently masculine or too feminine" (Berdahl et al., 1996: 343; Berdahl & Moore, 2006; Waldo et al., 1998; Berdahl & Moon, 2013: 343).

Men who wish to be actively involved in family life have been observed to voice concerns regarding being perceived as "wimpy and girlie" (McDowell, 2015: 3, citing Connell & Messerschmidt, 2005), a "sissy" (Kimmel, 1994: 119) and a "feminine man" (Locke, 2016: 199). It has been noted that fathers who relinquish paid work due to caregiving responsibilities are often subjected to teasing, both inside and outside of the workplace (Segal, 2006; Berdahl & Moon, 2013; Solomon, 2014;28). The film and TV industry provides many examples of caregiving fathers facing mockery, with family comedy films such as *Daddy Day-Care* and *What to Expect When You're Expecting* consistently mocking fathers when they display caregiving behaviours (Sunderland, 2006). More recent UK television comedies such as *Motherland* and *Catastrophe* portray caregiving fathers in a similar light. Such a portrayal is also observable in children's cartoons; for example, within *Peppa Pig*, 'Daddy Pig's' parenting endeavours are depicted as comedic, the same is true for Homer Simpson and earlier Fred Flintstone (Freed & Millar, 2018). Whilst not without exception, such populist representations can be observed to consistently transmit the message regarding what is acceptable behaviour for a father and what is not, portraying caregiving behaviour undertaken by fathers as a source of humour.

Academics have proposed that men who challenge stereotypical expectations of behaviour through active involvement in family life can expect to face judgements of disapproval from others (Doucet, 2006; Doucet & Merla, 2007). The disapproval has been observed to come from the direction of both male and female co-workers, albeit its nature seems to be gender dependent, with women found to perceive caregiving fathers as "merely wanting to get out of breadwinner obligations", and 'real men' feeling dislike towards them (Podnieks, 2016: 15). Other authors have identified that the disapproval of caregiving fathers by colleagues often takes the form of stigmatisation, prejudice and implicit and explicit workplace discrimination (Wayne & Cordeiro, 2003; Locke, 2016). Existing literatures are also indicative that fathers themselves often feel under pressure to be earning and believe that any deviation from breadwinning behaviours results in "social scrutiny", being "tinged with suspicion" and struggling for "social legitimacy" (Doucet & Merla, 2007: 363). Some of the challenges facing caregiving fathers can be considered to relate to a broader context than the workplace, with theorists noting a sense of social exclusion for such fathers in society more generally. For example, caregiving fathers have been observed to find attending activities with their children, such as playgroups as challenging. Fathers in this context have reported feeling 'ostracized' by the mothers in attendance which might explain why caregiving fathers often report a sense of isolation and social exclusion (Bird, 1996; Doucet, 2004; Sheridan, 2004; Merla, 2008; Berdahl & Moon, 2013; Locke, 2016).

The social challenges facing caregiving fathers have been identified from existing literature as potentially hindering paternal involvement and can perhaps explain the adherence to more traditional role-congruent patterns of full-time working hours for fathers (Berdahl & Moon, 2013). Such adherence is perhaps unsurprising as fathers who take a more egalitarian approach to parenting and amend their working patterns to enable it have been found to be rated as less professionally competent than fathers who work full-time. Similarly, caregiving fathers have expressed concerns about 'career death' when they amend working hours for caregiving and thus may maintain traditional patterns of employment for fear of a negative a reaction (Moss & Deven, 1999; Reeves, 2002, cited in Halford, 2006: 387; Brescoll & Uhlmann, 2005; Berdahl & Moon, 2013; Gatrell et al., 2014).

In the light of such mistreatment, it is unsurprising that for many fathers there is a tendency to adhere to traditional patterns of division of parental roles and work arrangements, and this will be explored in detail through the qualitative data obtained within the 'Fatherhood Forfeit Study' (Miller, 2010, cited by Gatrell & Cooper, 2016).

FATHERHOOD FORFEIT STUDY DATA

The qualitative data obtained from the 'Fatherhood Forfeit Study' which employed vignette-based focus groups with managers and semi-structured interviews with working parents and managers consistently demonstrated the 'Social Mistreatment of Caregiving Fathers' in both social and work settings. This theme comprises sub-themes identified on the basis of frequency and perceived importance expressed by the participants. The sub-themes are as follows; 'suspicion', facing 'negative judgement', 'mockery', 'struggling with friendships' and being 'viewed as idle'.

'Suspicion'

Evidence of the way in which fathers are viewed with 'suspicion' when they attempt to combine paid work with caregiving responsibilities was consistent in all elements of the qualitative data within the 'Fatherhood Forfeit Study'.

Within the vignette-based focus groups, manager participants were asked to discuss the suitability of the caregiving father applicant represented as an applicant applying for a part-time role. It was evidenced that some participants viewed his motivation for applying for a part-time role with 'suspicion':

I just wonder why he is applying for the job part-time … I wonder why? (Naval1)

But why would he (the father) be applying for a part-time role? (Naval2)

He is going from full-time to part-time, and we don't really know why. (NHS)

Such questioning regarding the choice of working arrangements of the mother applicant applying for the part-time role did not emerge in any of the focus groups. Within this climate, it is plausible that a father may feel that they are discouraged from prioritising childcare and thus revert to more traditional breadwinning norms (Miller, 2010; Tracy & Rivera, 2010).

Caregiving fathers being viewed with 'suspicion' also was evident in the working parent interviews, and was particularly prominent in households where the fathers worked reduced hours. Paul, a single part-time working father of one, explained the response to his working hours:

> I get a few funny faces, I get a few funny reactions ... people find it a little bit weird ... "oh, that's a bit weird, and that's a bit odd" ... I feel that any flexibility requested from a male in the workforce is treated with suspicion. In my opinion, I feel males are still seen as the non-contact parent; therefore, saying you want to reduce your hours (for a child related reason) is treated suspiciously.

Kelly, a full-time working mother whose partner worked part-time, echoed this experience and felt that the working hours of her partner are viewed with 'suspicion': "Both my brothers have expressed like "why isn't he doing more to support the family?" The phenomenon of caregiving fathers being viewed with 'suspicion' was also evident in interviews with managers. Jon, an HR manager, expressed that:

> It wouldn't surprise me if people would get cynical about a father working part-time in this environment ... they would struggle with part-time working for fathers, they would struggle to be open-minded about it.

Similarly, Mark, a senior manager, believed that caregiving fathers, particularly those who work part-time, are considered to be suspicious. He stated:

> They (part-time working fathers) are viewed with a great deal more suspicion, far more suspicion that a woman working part-time ... I think this would affect recruitment, as I expect at least one person on the panel (would be) viewing it as suspicious and viewing it as not normal. Men going part-time has been viewed with a lot of suspicion.

This effect is similar to that observed by Doucet and Merla in their work with Canadian stay-at-home fathers. Doucet and Merla observed that such fathers encountered 'social scrutiny' and interactions being 'tinged with suspicion' (Doucet & Merla, 2007; Doucet, 2009). This illustrates how judgements of suspicion can be seen to parallel a Canadian context to a UK context.

The notion of being viewed with 'suspicion' might explain the disparities in the ratings between the caregiving father applicant (depicted as an applicant for a part-time role) and the other parent applicants in the online vignette element of this study. It is plausible that the lower ratings assigned to the part-time father applicant may be a consequence of managers viewing the father with 'suspicion' which impacted negatively on the ratings assigned to this applicant. Conversely, judgements of 'suspicion' did not emerge in any element of the data for the mothers, pointing to this element of social mistreatment aligning exclusively to the behavioural expectations for fathers. Being viewed with 'suspicion' was not the only type of social mistreatment observed to be levied onto caregiving fathers within the 'Fatherhood Forfeit Study'. Fathers were also observed to face 'negative judgement' in their quest to take an active role in caregiving.

'Negative Judgement'

'Negative judgement' towards caregiving fathers emerged specifically with regard to fathers who wished to work part-time was widely apparent in all elements of the qualitative data, with the strongest impact being observable in the interviews with working parents as explored below.

Jack, who has two children and worked part-time whilst his children were pre-school age, expressed that "People could be fairly judgemental or at least seemed to be fairly judgemental about the working arrangement". Similarly, Kelly, a full-time working mother of one, felt her partner who worked part-time was judged negatively due to his working hours by her family, whom she believed were "disparaging about it – both my brothers are very, very, successful. They're very wealthy they would just fit all those kind of 'white male powerful criteria' ".

Corey, a married father of three, expressed how he would like to consider part-time working but was concerned about the social response. He stated, "I don't want to be one of those people Tuesdays, Wednesday And Thursday – they get called".

Sid, a father of four, who combined primary caregiving with self-employment and whose wife works full-time, recounted many examples of 'negative judgement' being directed at him. These included:

When people associate childcare with me it isn't a job ... the assumption is that it is a comedown, and I can't get a proper job.

Sid continued with a very poignant example of how he felt he was perceived negatively:

I wrote to the school about some concerns I had and asked for a meeting, they never got back to me, so I asked to meet with the governors and their view was very much 'there there little boy, you are just a dad who looks after your kids, you are not a proper person, you are not an upstanding citizen.'

A perception of 'negative judgement' can be aligned with the experience of full-time working mothers, who can be conceptualised as challenging traditional parental gender norms. However, it is noteworthy that 'negative judgement' towards mothers appeared to manifest themselves in slightly different ways to fathers and focused predominantly on judgements as a mother, rather than as a worker per se. For example Andrew, an NHS focus group participant, stated, "I'm not worried about employing a mother full-time; it is her kids that need to be worried". This view was echoed in the interviews with working parents and Caitlin, a full-time working mother of two who is married to a stay-at-home dad, stated that her choice to work full-time resulted in 'negative judgement' from her mother-in-law about her choice of working hours. "She thought it was disgusting that I had had children and gone back to work ... thought it was dreadful". Interestingly, 'negative judgement' regarding paternal full-time working hours did not emerge from the data. This can be linked to expectations regarding parental behaviour and assumptions of traditional patterns of employment, as mothers who work part-time also appeared to receive minimal 'negative judgement' regarding working hours.

This leads to the next theme of social mistreatment that emerged from the qualitative data which focuses around the issue of 'mockery'.

Mockery

The 'mockery' of caregiving fathers was evident in all elements of the qualitative data, with the characteristics of the mockery varying from blatant to innocuous. In the vignette-based manager focus group within a technology environment, the 'mockery' appeared quite light-hearted:

Participant A—*Is it perfectly acceptable for a father to want to spend time with his children in the same way as a mother?*

Participant B—*Depends if they like him or not. They might be saying no please don't stay home, get a job.*

They continued to mock the caregiving fathers, as illustrated by this quote:

Participant C—*"She probably needs the money because her husband's a caretaker. He ain't going to be bringing in a lot is he (laugh)".*

In the focus group in the charity sector, the 'mockery' was a little more ardent, and a comedic scenario was depicted when describing a caregiving father: *"He has got those kids ... strapped to his back while he's mowing the school playing field. He is sorted, happy, he is fine."*

In the line manager interviews, Dave reported that 'mockery' of caregiving fathers was also observable and suggested it takes the form of 'friendly banter':

I would say there would be friendly banter made towards a part-time father and probably some comments with menace ... in my most recent organisation, I would say that there would be 'friendly banter' but some vindictive comments are made behind people's backs depending on which area they worked in, production areas being the worst.

Similarly, Mark, a senior manager, believed that caregiving fathers face a considerable amount of 'mockery' in the workplace. He stated:

There would be a lot of piss taking ... 'You are a bit of a wuss', 'she rules the roost' 'wears the trousers' that sort of thing. If it (the working part-time) was due to childcare, I don't think it would be malicious, but I think there would definitely be an element of piss taking 'you are not a real man', 'what is wrong with your wife' ... it would be gentle, but it would definitely occur.

Sid, a father of four, who combined primary caregiving with self-employment and whose wife works full-time, narrated an example of the 'mockery' he received which seems in contrast to the 'gentle mockery' discussed by Mark and Dave:

A man I knew joked to me, 'who are you anyway? Well, you are just a bum really aren't you.' I did not take it as a joke.

The data presented under the heading of 'mockery' can be seen to range from what has been termed as 'friendly banter' to stronger more pointed types of 'mockery' with varying degrees of perceived severity. Not being taken seriously and being mocked could explain the ratings for the caregiving father depicted as a part-time father applicant in the quantitative online vignette survey element of the study. Additionally, it offers potential explanation for adherence to breadwinning norms for many fathers, a route that might be perceived to avoid the 'mockery' encountered by the participants of this study.

As indicated earlier in this chapter, the concept of caregiving fathers facing 'mockery' has been observed in previous studies, in which caregiving fathers have been found to be regularly subjected to teasing and name calling (Kerfoot & Knights, 1993; Collinson & Hearn, 1994; Kimmel & Mahler, 2003; Gregory, 2009; Solomon, 2014). It is interesting to note that with the exception of Solomon (2014), much of the research in this area is over 10 years old and some over 20 years old and the findings of this study are indicative that little has changed with regard to the associations of caregiving fatherhood and 'mockery'. A finding which is perhaps somewhat surprising given the UK climate of purported societal change regarding the conceptualisation of fatherhood along with government interventions through legislation, highlighting that there is significant progress still to be made. As with the sub-theme of 'suspicion', facing actual or perceived 'mockery' is proposed as a potential contributing factor in explaining the UK's adherence to the breadwinner model.

'Struggling with friendships'

This sub-theme was not widely apparent in the qualitative data from the 'Fatherhood Forfeit Study'. Nevertheless, the argument as to its inclusion is persuasive due to the impact it has on the fathers who were interviewed, therefore it seems appropriate to explore as a sub-theme. This theme specifically refers to the experience of fathers who felt that their friendships were more complex as a result of their active involvement in caregiving responsibilities.

Sue, a full-time working mother of two, outlined the experience of her husband who worked part-time:

Oh, he found it really difficult ... he had two young kids and the network wasn't really there and he missed his friends ... He did struggle for a long while. He didn't really mix with very many other fathers ... there was a big group of fathers (who worked full-time) that made really good friends with each other. He didn't become part of that group ... he's not one of them ... he could have been but they've never invited him.

Very similar friendship issues were experienced first-hand by Sid, a father of four, who combined primary caregiving with self-employment and whose wife works full-time.

I didn't go to too many playgroups, I didn't really want to face it. I didn't want to go in as the only guy. Some are more welcoming than others, but with some women, I think there is always a horrible undertone .... I have probably not helped myself, the more I resisted it the more isolated I got.. it was a bear pit ... I felt excluded.

This also extended to his social circle outside of the children:

I don't go to xxxx social gatherings. Generally when people ask me "what I do?", there is a blank expression nothing tangible a man can get hold of largely, and I have always found that quite difficult. It is always the first thing people say, I never ask people as I don't want them to ask me .... It is having that hook, and I think it is the hook of work .... I have become a bit detached from the mainstream group of friends; I have friends who I have known for years but not really many around here. I felt excluded ...

Similarly, Mark, a senior manager, also believed that caregiving fathers would face a struggle with friendships, however, he was more positive and states that whilst fathers "would not be initially part of the main group but over time I don't think it would be a problem".

The findings within this sub-theme support existing literature in this area, as many academics have observed caregiving fathers 'struggling with friendships'; however, data from a contemporary UK context are a little sparse and thus the 'Fatherhood Forfeit Study' extends existing knowledge in this area (Bird, 1996; Petre, 1998: 216; Doucet, 2004; Merla, 2008; Berdahl & Moon, 2013; Locke, 2016). It is pertinent to note that the majority of the data from this theme emerged from social settings other than specifically the workplace; therefore, how much this theme translates into workplace practices or indeed impacts upon workplace decision-making is unclear. The final sub-theme is more closely inter-twined with the workplace, focusing on the work ethic of caregiving fathers and a belief that fathers who wish to be actively involved in the caregiving of their children are perceived in a less favourable way than fathers who align to more traditional conceptualisations of breadwinners.

'Viewed as idle'

The final sub-theme of 'viewed as idle' within the theme of social mistreat-ment was most prominent in the vignette-based focus group discussions, with elements also emerging to a slightly lesser degree within the semi-structured interviews with managers and working parents. Within the focus group in the technology environment, the caregiving father depicted in the vignette was described as, "dozy". Similarly, in the same focus group, questions were raised about the character of the caregiving father applicant, represented as an applicant for a part-time role: "Is he a high-flyer?" and "Is he slower off the mark?" Such comments imply that the fictitious applicant might have limited ambition, and it is challenging to disentangle this from his choice of working hours as a consequence of his caregiving responsibilities, particularly, as such statements were not made about either of the mother applicants. Participants in the focus group within the charity sector embarked on a broader discussion, moving away from the vignette, and a forceful statement was made about fathers who work part-time generally:

> There are few of them at my kids' school, I know it works for some families as she earns more than him etc. but every time I see them, I just think, go to work – lazy bastard – it wouldn't work for my house.

This is further illustrated through quotes from interviews with both working fathers and managers when discussing the workplace response if a father needed to leave work for caregiving responsibilities. They included:

> "How convenient, you're not available to work again!"; "Are you off again, you've only just arrived"; "Nice of you to turn up"; "Do you pay your son to be sick?" (Paul, a divorced father of one)

> *"Taking early retirement are we?"; "you work-shy f****r".* (Dave, Line Manager)

Each of these statements imply an impeded work ethic, and such perceptions of caregiving fathers are in line with existing research from over 20 years ago in the US which also found fathers to be criticised more than mothers for doing too little paid work (Etaugh & Folger, 1998; Deutsch & Saxon, 1998); this effect is particularly evident for stay-at-home fathers who have been viewed as 'good for nothing' when they relinquished paid work (Vandello et al., 2008). This sub-theme demonstrated that this specific area of social mistreatment remains in existence over time, overcoming geographic barriers by translating to a UK context. If caregiving fathers are conceptualised as 'idle', then it is likely to have an impact on how they are rated during the selection process, and this can be considered to be a potential contributory factor in the maintenance of the UK societal norm of full-time, breadwinning father rather than pathways which might allow for a more active role in caregiving.

CHAPTER SUMMARY

This chapter has explored the fatherhood forfeit of the 'Social Mistreatment of Caregiving Fathers' through exploring both the existing academic terrain and qualitative data from the 'Fatherhood Forfeit Study' that pertains to this area. In a general sense, this theme affirms the findings of Berdahl and Moon (2013), as the social mistreatment of men who violate traditional gender roles observed in their 2013 US study was also widely observable in all elements of the qualitative data within the 'Fatherhood Forfeit Study'. However, this fatherhood forfeit also builds upon existing knowledge through providing more detail as to the type of social mistreatment experienced by caregiving fathers in a UK context from the viewpoint of managers and working parents. Specifically, this is achieved through the development of the sub-themes of 'suspicion', 'negative judgement', 'mockery', 'struggling with friendships' and being 'viewed as idle' by way of explaining the mistreatment faced by caregiving fathers. It is suggested that fear of facing, or actually facing, social mistreatment might result in fathers shying away from active involvement in caregiving, rejecting work patterns to facilitate such involvement and remaining in full-time work. It is also proposed that sub-themes such as 'suspicion' and 'viewed as idle' may also contribute to an explanation of disparities in the ratings of the caregiving father depicted as a part-time applicant in the online vignette survey element of this study. It is suggested that an environment of 'social mistreatment' might push caregiving fathers towards maintenance of breadwinning norms in an attempt to either avoid this, or as a consequence of it.

REFERENCES

Berdahl, J. L. (2007). The sexual harassment of uppity women. *Journal of Applied Psychology, 92*(2), 425–437. Available at: https://pdfs.semanticscholar.org/a389/10a5779c36806c509b3725c093b501fd1a7d.pdf.   Accessed   28 Sept 2018.

Berdahl, J. L., & Moon, S. H. (2013). Workplace mistreatment of middle class workers based on sex, parenthood and caregiving. *Journal of Social Issues, 69*(2), 341–366. https://doi.org/10.1111/josi.12018

Berdahl, J. L., & Moore, C. (2006). Workplace harassment: Double jeopardy for minority women. *Journal of Applied Psychology, 91*(2), 426–436. Available at: https://pdfs.semanticscholar.org/c5cd/8934b5d10b331560b24bcc3d7dc3c4a4818d.pdf. Accessed 28 Sept 2018.

Berdahl, J. L., Magley, V. J., & Waldo, C. R. (1996). The sexual harassment of men?: Exploring the concept with theory and data. *Psychology of Women Quarterly, 20*(4), 527–547. https://doi.org/10.1111/j.1471-6402.1996.tb00320.x

Bird, S. R. (1996). Welcome to the men's club: Homosociality and the maintenance of hegemonic masculinity. *Gender & Society, 10*(2), 120–132. https://doi.org/10.1177/089124396010002002

Brescoll, V. L., & Uhlmann, E. L. (2005). Attitudes toward traditional and nontraditional parents. *Psychology of Women Quarterly, 29*(4), 436–445. Available at: http://www.socialjudgments.com/docs/Brescoll%20and%20Uhlmann%202005.pdf. Accessed 28 Sept 2018.

Burnett, S. B., Gatrell, C. J., Cooper, C. L., & Sparrow, P. (2013). Fathers at work: A ghost in the organizational machine. *Gender, Work and Organization, 20*(6), 632–646. https://doi.org/10.1111/gwao.12000

Collinson, D., & Hearn, J. (1994). Naming men as men: Implications for work, organization and management. *Gender, Work and Organization, 1*(1), 2–22.

Connell, R. (1987). *Gender and power: Society, the person, and sexual politics.* Stanford University Press.

Connell, R. W., & Messerschmidt, J. W. (2005). Hegemonic masculinity: Rethinking the concept. *Gender & Society, 19*(6), 829–859.

Correll, S., Benard, S., & Paik, I. (2007). Getting a job: Is there a motherhood penalty? *American Journal of Sociology, 112*(5), 1297–1338.

Cuddy, A. C., Fiske, S. T., & Glick, P. (2004). When professionals become mothers, warmth doesn't cut the ice. *Journal of Social Issues, 60*(4), 701–718. https://doi.org/10.1111/j.0022-4537.2004.00381.x

Deutsch, F. M., & Saxon, S. E. (1998). Traditional ideologies, non-traditional lives. *Sex Roles, 38*(5/6), 331–362.

Doucet, A. (2004). It's almost like I have a job, but I don't get paid: Fathers at home reconfiguring work, care, and masculinity. *Fathering, 2*(3), 277–303.

Doucet, A. (2006). *Do men mother?: Fathering, care, and domestic responsibility*. University of Toronto Press.

Doucet, A. (2009). Dad and baby in the first year: Gendered responsibilities and embodiment. *The Annals of the American Academy of Political and Social Science, 624*(1), 78–98.

Doucet, A., & Merla, L. (2007). Stay-at-home fathering: A strategy for balancing work and home in Canadian and Belgian families. *Community, Work & Family, 10*(4), 455–473.

Duffy, M. K., Ganster, D. C., Shaw, J. D., Johnson, J. L., & Pagon, M. (2006). The social context of undermining behavior at work. *Organizational Behavior and Human Decision Processes, 101*(1), 105–126.

Etaugh, C., & Folger, D. (1998). Perceptions of parents whose work and parenting behaviours deviate from role expectations. *Sex Roles, 39*(3), 215–223.

Freed, D., & Millar, J. (2018). *Dads don't babysit- towards equal parenting*. Ortus Press.

Fuegen, K., Biernat, M., Haines, E., & Deaux, K. (2004). Mothers and fathers in the workplace: How gender and parental status influence judgments of job-related competence. *Journal of Social Issues, 60*(4), 737–754.

Gatrell, C., & Cooper, C. L. (2016). A sense of entitlement? Fathers, mothers and organizational support for family and career. *Community, Work & Family, 19*(2), 134–147.

Gatrell, C. J., Burnett, S. B., Cooper, C. L., & Sparrow, P. (2014). Parents, perceptions and belonging: Exploring flexible working among UK fathers and mothers. *British Journal of Management, 25*(3), 473–487.

Gregory, M. R. (2009). Inside the locker room: Male homosociability in the advertising industry. *Gender, Work and Organization, 16*(3), 323–347.

Gruber, J. E. (1998). The impact of male work environments and organizational policies on women's experiences of sexual harassment. *Gender & Society, 12*(3), 301–320.

Halford, S. (2006). Collapsing the boundaries? Fatherhood, organization and home-working. *Gender, Work and Organization, 13*(4), 383–402.

Hersch, J., & Stratton, L. S. (2000). Household specialization and the male marriage wage premium. *Industrial and Labor Relations Review, 54*(1), 78–94. https://doi.org/10.1177/001979390005400105

Kerfoot, D., & Knights, D. (1993). Management, masculinity and manipulation: From paternalism to corporate strategy in financial services in Britain. *Journal of Management Studies, 30*(4), 659–677.

Kimmel, M. (1994). Masculinity as homophobia: Fear, shame and silence in the construction of gender identity. In H. Brod & M. Kaufman (Eds.), *Theorising masculinities* (pp. 119–142). Sage.

Kimmel, M. S., & Mahler, M. (2003). Adolescent masculinity, homophobia, and violence: Random school shootings', 1982-200. *American Behavioral Scientist, 46*(10), 1439–1458.

Lamb, M. E. (2004). *The role of the father in child development.* Wiley.

Locke, A. (2016). Masculinity, subjectivities, and caregiving in the British press: The case of the stay-at-home father. In E. Podnieks (Ed.), *Pops in pop culture* (pp. 195–212). Palgrave Macmillan.

Loh, E. S. (1996). Productivity and the marriage premium for white males. *Journal of Human Resources, 31*(3), 566–589. http://www.jstor.org/stable/i301295

McDowell, T. (2015). *Applying critical social theories to family therapy practice.* Springer.

Merla, L. (2008). Determinants, costs, and meanings of Belgian stay-at-home fathers: An international comparison. *Fathering, 6*(2), 113–132. Available at: http://www.mensstudies.info/OJS/index.php/FATHERING/article/view/280. Accessed 28 Sept 2018.

Miller, T. (2010). *Making sense of fatherhood: Gender, caring and work.* Cambridge University Press.

Moss, P., & Deven, F. (Eds.). (1999). *Parental leave: Progress or pitfall? Research and policy issues in Europe, 35.* NDID/CGBS Publications.

Petre, D. (1998). *Father time: Making time for your children.* Pan Macmillan.

Pleck, E. H., & Pleck, J. H. (1997). Fatherhood ideals in the United States: Historical dimensions. In M. E. Lamb (Ed.), *The role of the father in child development* (3rd ed., pp. 33–48). Wiley.

Podnieks, E. (Ed.). (2016). *Pops in pop culture* (pp. 1–27). Palgrave Macmillan.

Reeves, R. (2002). *Dad's army: The case for father-friendly workplaces.* The Work Foundation.

Ridgeway, C., & Correll, S. J. (2004). Motherhood as a status characteristic. *Journal of Social Issues, 60*(4), 683–700. https://doi.org/10.1111/j.0022-4537.2004.00380.x

Rudman, L. A., & Mescher, K. (2013). Penalizing men who request a family leave: Is flexibility stigma a femininity stigma? *Journal of Social Issues, 69*(2), 322–340.

Segal, L. (2006). *Slow motion: Changing masculinities, changing men* (3rd ed.). Palgrave Macmillan.

Sheridan, A. (2004). Chronic presenteeism: The multiple dimensions to men's absence from part time work. *Gender, Work and Organization, 11*(2), 207–225.

Solomon, C. R. (2014). 'After months of it, you just want to punch someone in the face': Stay-at-home fathers and masculine identities. *Michigan Family Review, 18*(1), 23–38. https://doi.org/10.3998/mfr.4919087.0018.103

Sunderland, J. (2006). 'Parenting' or 'mothering'? The case of modern childcare magazines. *Discourse & Society, 17*(4), 503–528. https://doi.org/10.1177/0957926506063126

Tracy, S. J., & Rivera, K. D. (2010). Endorsing equity and applauding stay-at-home moms: How male voices on work-life reveal aversive sexism and flickers of transformation. *Management Communication Quarterly, 24*(1), 3–43. https://doi.org/10.1177/0893318909352248

Vandello, J. A., Bosson, J. K., Cohen, D., Burnaford, R. M., & Weaver, J. R. (2008). Precarious manhood. *Journal of Personality and Social Psychology, 95*(6), 1325–1339. https://doi.org/10.1037/a0012453

Waldo, C. R., Berdahl, J. L., & Fitzgerald, L. F. (1998). Are men sexually harassed? If so, by whom? *Law and Human Behavior, 22*(1), 59–79.

Wayne, J. H., & Cordeiro, B. L. (2003). Who is a good organizational citizen? Social perception of male and female employees who use family leave. *Sex Roles, 49*(5–6), 233–246.

CHAPTER 6

What Is Next for Caregiving Fathers?

Abstract This final chapter explores the practical steps that organisations can take to minimise the 'fatherhood forfeits' as presented in this book, through identification of specific organisational actions, reference to exemplars in this area and wider academic research.

This chapter would be incomplete without reference to the impact of the Covid-19 pandemic on family life during which time many parents found it necessary to undertake largely unaltered working schedules with minimal access to their usual support mechanisms, including schools, nurseries and more informal sources of support such as grandparents (ONS, *Coronavirus and employment for parents in the UK*, 2020; Sevilla & Smith, *Baby steps: The gender division of childcare during the COVID19 pandemic*. IZA DP IZA Institute of Labor Economics, 2020).

The 'Fatherhood Forfeit Study' has many potential implications for how caregiving fathers are conceptualised and treated within the workplace. Raising awareness of these at both the macro and micro levels is critical if their experience is to be improved, discrimination minimised and ultimately working life improved for both mothers and fathers.

Keywords Fathers • Discrimination • Unconscious bias • Flexible Working • Organisational/Workplace Support • Covid 19

IMPACT OF THE PANDEMIC FOR FATHERS

For many families, a consequence of the Covid-19 lockdowns is that paternity has become a more 'immersive experience', resulting in a reduction of the gender gap of childcare hours between mothers and fathers (Cito et al., 2020: 252; Sevilla & Smith, 2020). During this period, typical patterns of women routinely undertaking the lion's share of caregiving were disrupted for many families bringing with it observable increases in gender equality (Henz, 2017; Sevilla & Smith, 2020).

Academic research emerging from the pandemic suggests that the Covid-19 lockdowns resulted in two main changes for fathers: a change in fathers themselves, and a change in how organisations view them. Firstly, it is suggested by some that the increased time that many fathers spent with their children as a consequence of the pandemic resulted in them becoming increasingly aware of the needs of their children and gaining a greater understanding "about what kids are actually doing all day" (Burrell & Ruxton, 2020; Shafer et al., 2020; Alon et al., 2020: 21). As a consequence of this and broader experiences during the lockdowns, many families appear to be re-evaluating their work-life balance and are looking to make permanent changes to their working arrangements, learning the value of changes to work routines to allow for wider involvement in family life (Kelland et al., 2020). Furthermore, according to the Fatherhood Institute report 'Locked Down Fathers - The Untold Story', fathers grew in confidence, learnt new skills, built stronger relationships with their children and their parenting has improved during the pandemic (Burgess, 2021a).

Secondly, and most relevant to the focus of this book, the pandemic, for many, has resulted in an increased awareness of family needs within the employment relationship, with employers and co-workers becoming more aware of the childcare needs of their colleagues (Alon et al., 2020). More specifically for fathers, it has been suggested that the pandemic has resulted in a deviation away from work cultures in which a father's paid work is unaltered by fatherhood (Andrew et al., 2020). Some academics are predicting long-lasting impacts on gender equality, an increasing number of parents wanting to take a more active role in the caregiving of their children as a consequence of their experiences during the pandemic, creating a potential "silver lining" to the pandemic (Forbes et al., 2021; Andrew et al., 2020: 27; Chung et al., 2020). This is supported by Jane van Zyl, Chief Executive Officer of Working Families, who stated:

> The pandemic has been a big wakeup call for many fathers and partners about what they want their role to be in raising their children in the future.

As we build back after the pandemic it is in every employers' interest to make sure their workplace culture and employee benefits support fathers to get a good work life balance and allows them to play a meaningful role in their children's lives from the start. (van Zyl, 2021)

Addressing the 'fatherhood forfeits' as identified in this book is envisaged to be a key tool to enable working parents to harness the impact of the pandemic, which for many families resulted in an increased paternal involvement in caregiving.

This book now moves to explore the changes that can be made at the organisational level through exploring workplace practice and the available academic research in this area. In addition, reference is made to potential areas of change at the macro level towards the end of the chapter.

ORGANISATIONAL ACTIONS FROM THE FATHERHOOD FORFEIT STUDY

The study presented within this book has highlighted specific challenges faced by caregiving fathers when they attempt to take an active role in the parenting of their children which have been identified as the 'fatherhood forfeits'. It is suggested that 'fatherhood forfeits' may act as a barrier to fathers taking an active role in caregiving which may negatively impact upon the fathers themselves, their families and ultimately might have a part to play in the continuation of the gender pay gap which peaks when adults become parents. To reduce the disparities identified within the 'Fatherhood Forfeit Study', there are a number of potential interventions that could be employed within organisations. This chapter focuses on six potential areas of organisational action: specifically, organisational policy and leave, the role of leaders and managers, monitoring, mentoring, organisational training and fatherhood forums. Naturally, this list of potential interventions is not exhaustive, but these specific actions have been focused upon due to their prominence in both the academic and the organisational arenas.

Organisational Policy and Leave

A central way to support caregiving fathers in the workplace and minimise the 'fatherhood forfeits' as identified within this book is suggested to be through equalising parental leave provision, with mandatory paternity leave periods that are non-transferable and 'use it or lose it' parental leave entitlements are highlighted as having a key role in the equalising of parental load in the post pandemic workplace (Mangiavacchi et al., 2021; King et al., 2020). This is advocated by Adrienne Burgess, Joint Chief Executive of the Fatherhood Institute, who reports that "It's imperative that workplaces visibly and systematically support fathers' caretaking. This will include offering every new parent, male or female, a period of well-paid non-transferable leave for caretaking in the first year after their baby's birth; supporting flexible working (time and place) wherever possible" (Burgess, 2021b).

An example of a company that has taken this approach is Aviva, who have a strong reputation for leading the way with regard to improving the workplace experience of fathers, including offering both parents 26 weeks' parental leave on full pay (Aviva, 2021). They report that 99% of new dads in 2020 took parental leave, with the average leave amount taken by fathers in 2020 being 24 weeks; a number that is increasing year on year. John Lewis have followed this pattern and introduced six months' paid leave for mothers and fathers in 2021 (The Guardian, 2021). Such employer interventions are identified by award winning blogger John Adams from DadBlog (www.dadblog.com) as being a key way for employers to support fathers, suggesting that the allocation of paid leave to mothers alone "looks incredibly old fashioned and says a lot about the working culture" (Adams, 2021a).

Such equalisation of the organisational leave policy for parents is likely to impact upon a reduction in the potential for 'fatherhood forfeits' to occur through altering the climate from one of negotiation, that is fraught with challenges and bias, to one of entitlement. Specifically, with regard to the theme of the 'Social Mistreatment of Caregiving Fathers' and notions of fathers being 'conceptualised as idle' and viewed with 'suspicion', there is potential for such stereotyping to be minimised if entitlement to leave is equalised and access to it becomes more commonplace for fathers as well as mothers. In addition, it might reduce the forfeit of 'fathers obtaining less workplace support', through weakening the automatic assumptions that associate mothers with children as evidenced within the theme of 'Think Child–Think Mum'.

It is suggested by Forbes and Birkett within their 'Fathers in the Workplace Toolkit' that fathers in particular often "feel nervous about asking to use policies such as shared parental leave and paternity leave" (Forbes & Birkett, 2020). This aligns to the findings of the 'Fatherhood Forfeit Study', in which fathers were found to 'obtain less workplace support for caregiving than mothers' and face social mistreatment in their quest, suggesting the notion of 'nervousness' is well founded. They continue that organisations need to have a clear policy in place which situates the leave allocation within company-wide parenting policies which are easy to access on the company intranet, incorporated into managers training and widely publicised internally. Such actions are critical to ensure that all staff are fully aware of their entitlements and to demonstrate that organisations have an authentic commitment to supporting both mothers and fathers in the workplace.

A specific approach to organisational policy that can support caregiving fathers in the workplace and minimise 'fatherhood forfeits' is to adopt flexible working policies. It has been identified in the 'Fatherhood Forfeit Study' that caregiving fathers are less likely to obtain a role that is conducive to caregiving (such as part-time work), and that more generally, fathers 'obtain less organisational support for caregiving'. This is also evident within organisations in a broader sense, as even companies, such as Aviva, who are known for widely supporting working fathers observe that women returning from parental leave were more likely to request a formal change to their work pattern than men (Aviva, 2021). However, it is possible that the Covid-19 pandemic might go some way to reduce some of these fatherhood forfeits by strengthening the case for access to flexible working, due to changing perceptions, albeit tentative, of working fathers during the pandemic (Alon et al., 2020).

It has been found that during this period, employers and colleagues have gained a greater understanding that both mothers and fathers may require more flexibility to balance paid work with childcare (Andrew et al., 2020). This is supported by the Fatherhood Institute report entitled 'Lockdown Fathers - The Untold Story' which highlights that as organisations emerge from the Covid-19 context it is increasingly important to be explicit in organisational policies and internal communications that flexible working options are available to men as well as women with the aim of normalising men's uptake (Burgess, 2021a). This is supported by Jane Van Zyl, Chief Executive Officer of Working Families, who states that organisations need to be "loud and proud about the benefits they offer to their male employees who are fathers or want to start a family" and that this action is central to the attraction and retention of diverse, talented staff in the aftermath of the pandemic (van Zyl, 2021). Furthermore, this has been evidenced with data from early findings of a study undertaken by Kelland et al. (2020) that investigated the experiences of working parent couples during the Covid-19 lockdown period in the UK. It was observed that the pandemic resulted in a reduction of some of the challenges faced by fathers in obtaining flexibility. For example, 'Sarah' reported that whilst her partner's company had always been very resistant to flexible and home working, "they are finally seeing how it can work". Furthermore, it was reported by 'Alice' that company perceptions on work-life balance transformed during this period. She stated, "suddenly oh yes, people have a family … maybe it feels a bit more culturally acceptable" (Kelland et al., 2020).

Wider access for fathers to flexible working policies has been identified as having a central role in enabling a more equal division of caregiving responsibilities in both the pre- and post-Covid workplace (Chung et al., 2020 citing Langner, 2018; Chung & Van der Horst, 2020; National Working Families Report, 2019, APLEN, 2019). Certainly, it appears that the argument for flexible working has gathered significant momentum during the pandemic, with an ongoing increase in remote working and virtual meetings expected to continue long after the pandemic (Alon et al., 2020; Andrew et al., 2020). In support of this, it is observable that initiatives such as the #flexforall and #flexappeal campaigns came to the fore during the pandemic, highlighting the mutually beneficial nature of flexibility for both parents. Such campaigns place emphasis on the importance of establishing a model of flexible working as a 'day-one' right for all, with the aim of reducing gender inequality. As mentioned earlier with regard to policy and leave, such systems move the process of requesting flexible working away from the complex network of favours and negotiation that often guides decision-making in this area. This move towards automatic entitlement is likely to have a specific impact on the 'fatherhood forfeit' of fathers 'obtaining less workplace support than mothers' and being less likely to secure a role that allows for the combination of caregiving and working, such as a part-time role as was evident in the online vignette element of the 'Fatherhood Forfeit Study'.

Finally, with regard to policy in a more general sense, if organisations are to minimise the potential for 'fatherhood forfeits', attention needs to be paid to all elements of the employment relationship. In particular, a review of all policies in relation to recruitment, selection, and promotion processes to explore areas of potential bias and discrimination towards caregiving fathers. These should specifically focus on the minimisation of the occurrence of 'fatherhood forfeits' related to fathers not obtaining working arrangements conducive to caregiving through ensuring that requests from fathers for non-standard hours (which deviate from the full-time breadwinning norm) are addressed fairly, and steps are taken to avoid errors in organisational recruitment, selection and promotion decision-making. Additionally, with regard to the forfeit of the 'Social Mistreatment of Caregiving Fathers', attention needs to be paid to bullying and harassment policies to ensure that they encompass this element of discrimination. As indicated earlier, the 'fatherhood forfeit' of 'mockery' within the social mistreatment theme often emerged as 'light-hearted banter'. However, it is suggested that organisations adopt a zero-tolerance policy against such micro-aggressions to minimise the transmission of a message which implies that being a caregiving father is not culturally acceptable.

Whilst organisational policy has a key role to play in the shifting of organisational norms surrounding fatherhood, it can be considered to be largely ineffectual without clear communication of such policies throughout management structures (Forbes & Birkett, 2020). This can be achieved through the introduction of management training focused on both information provision and exploring attitudes towards family-friendly policies. For example, international law firm Hill Dickinson was commended in the Working Families Best Practice Awards for the way in which it specifically trains all managers in how to manage flexible working (Working Families, Best Practice Awards, 2020). Within the online vignette survey element of the 'Fatherhood Forfeit Study', it was clearly apparent that managers judged the caregiving father, depicted as a part-time father applicant, more harshly than any other working parent scenarios. Specific manager training to address this discrimination at the point of selection is likely to result in a reduction of such bias and increase awareness of the challenges facing caregiving fathers, resulting in them obtaining a more equal amount of workplace support in a more general sense. Such line manager training regarding flexible working policies and the identification of their benefits is becoming increasingly important and has been highlighted as being a central way that organisations can manage in the post-Covid-19 recovery period (Chung et al., 2020). This is coming to the fore as there are now labour shortages in some sectors post-Brexit making retention of skilled staff increasingly important.

In addition to undertaking training, managers and leaders can support caregiving fathers in the workplace through active role modelling. Having senior leaders who are active and positive role models has been identified as a central tool in encouraging the uptake of family-friendly policies such as SPL (Government Equalities Office, 2020). John Adams from Dadblog.

com supports this organisational action by emphasising the importance of senior managers actively encouraging dialogue regarding the management of the balance between work and caring responsibilities. He states:

> Having board members back at their desks two days after the arrival of a child is not a good look, and staff are looking to the example set by senior managers about how to behave. (Adams, 2021a)

The active display by senior staff of fathering practices that move away from the breadwinner model transmits a message that this is both acceptable and encouraged within the organisation. Specifically, such organisational role modelling can be conceptualised as a mechanism by which the 'fatherhood forfeit' of 'Think Mum–Think Child' can be reduced, demonstrating how the senior team themselves are not automatically aligning caregiving responsibilities solely to mothers. Additionally, such active role modelling from senior staff has the potential to reduce the social mistreatment element of the 'fatherhood forfeit'. In particular it is likely to reduce the forfeits of 'conceptualisations of being idle' and viewed with 'suspicion' through establishing that wider involvement in caregiving is socially acceptable.

Monitoring

As with any organisational intervention intended to improve the working life of their staff, ongoing monitoring is always going to be a key tool (Harrington et al., 2017). For example, companies such as the National Grid monitor the effectiveness of their parenting programmes to ensure consistency (Working Families Best Practice Awards, 2015). As intimated earlier, as organisations emerge from the pandemic, it is likely there will be an increase in the demand from fathers wanting to opt for more flexible working patterns due to positive experiences during this period (Kelland et al., 2020).

Sarah Jackson, OBE, a leading expert on work-life balance and family-friendly working and visiting professor at Cranfield University, concurs with this and states:

> Monitoring is essential. Organisations need to be able to count their father population and track their progress. To know how many take leave and work flexibly, and how many do not, understand those choices and to track per-

formance and promotions, comparing and contrasting within the male and the general populations. (Jackson, 2021)

Thus, the need for ongoing monitoring of the prevalence of 'fatherhood forfeits' is necessary, specifically regarding the effectiveness of organisational support for caregiving and access to working arrangements that facilitate caregiving. In keeping with this it is suggested by the Fatherhood Institute in their report entitled 'Lockdown Fathers – The Untold Story' (Burgess, 2021a) that specific annual monitoring on staff working flexibly (by gender, ethnicity and seniority in job role) is a central component in increasing parental equality after the pandemic.

Mentoring

Mentoring has been noted by many as a central way to shift organisational norms to a position of gender equality for both parents, and thus acts as a potential way to reduce the impact of the 'fatherhood forfeits' as identified in this book. For example, Brad Harrington and colleagues from the Boston College Centre for Work and Family (2017) observe that voluntary mentoring programmes for fathers that explore work-family dilemmas and the challenges men face, in addition to career-related discussions, can be key in helping fathers reduce conflict between work and life satisfaction. Similarly, Ian Dinwiddy, Founder and Director of the www.inspiringdads.co.uk website, observes that such programmes create "a supportive space to articulate, understand and plan for the particular pressures that fathers face in a complicated world, improving well-being, relationships with partners and children and delivering broader equality benefits at work and at home" (Dinwiddy, 2021).

It was identified in the Working Families Best Practice Awards (2021) that mentoring and coaching can be key tools in improving the experience of fathers within the workplace, and it highlighted how the Scottish Parliament embrace this notion through the establishment of a parental mentoring scheme open to women and men who wish to take extended leave. This can be likened to the approach taken by Nestle who have established 'Parent Pals', a peer-to-peer mentoring network across all of its offices (Nestle, 2021). Such an in-house approach can involve the deployment of 'Working Dad Champions' who are visible and approachable men who can mentor other male employees and explain how they balance work and family life (Adams, 2021a).

For some companies, an external mentoring approach is preferred. For example, British Land successfully adopted an external mentoring system for their employees who are fathers, providing those who take shared parental leave with up to 12 hours of external parental coaching per child. It is reported by Charlotte Whitley, Head of Communications, that both their business and employees have seen numerous benefits, which include an improved handover between employees before and after a period of leave, the building and maintenance of supportive networks within the organisation, an opportunity to address anxieties about returning to work following shared parental leave and a greater ability to find and maintain a balance between home and work (Whitley, 2021).

Such mentoring programmes can be conceptualised as a potential way of reducing 'fatherhood forfeits' through encouragement of explicit discussions of the challenges faced by individual caregiving fathers in the workplace, to explore strategies to overcome them and to seek support in dealing with them.

Organisational Training

The 'Fatherhood Forfeit Study' has outlined that the workplace experience for caregiving fathers is fraught with challenges, and for many, this results in the continuation of more traditional patterns of organising work and family. Thus, organisational training that directly addresses these barriers emerges as an appropriate workplace intervention and was identified as a key mechanism by which to support working fathers by many of the organisations that were featured in the Working Families Best Practice Awards (2021). It was highlighted within these awards how global investment banking firm Citi run 'New Dads Workshops' that provides practical advice on paternity leave, pay, flexible working, childcare, healthcare, how to manage boundaries and the changing role of the father. For some organisations, such as the London School of Economics, these workshops are open to not only their employees but also are extended to the partners of their employees (Working Families, Best Practice Awards, 2015). As with mentoring, not all workplaces run such workshops in-house and therefore enlist support from external companies such as Mindful Return (https://www.mindfulreturn.com/) who offer specific training courses for working fathers which they can engage with either independently or via their organisations to help support employees. Its founder, Lori Mihalich-Levin, reports that "the opportunity to have a structured curriculum around the transition to fatherhood and to engage with others at a similar life stage leaves course alumni feeling less isolated and more confident about their evolving identities". She continues that employers who offer this type of training programme have seen dramatically improved new parent retention statistics (Mihalich-Levin, 2021).

Such an approach is supported by Harrington et al. (2017), who advocate it as a key tool in helping fathers navigate the career-life challenges they are faced with, helping them to clearly identify the source of their conflicts and ways to resolve them. It is suggested by this book that such workshops are expanded to include exploration of 'fatherhood forfeits', to raise awareness of the issues observed in this book and to enable discussions of how to mitigate them.

More generally, it is apparent that wider training for all staff that focuses on the challenges facing caregiving fathers in the workplace is established. Such training could specifically explore the impacts of the 'fatherhood forfeits', so that employees can both recognise and challenge them. A potential way of achieving this aim is through alignment with existing unconscious bias training. Traditional unconscious bias training tends to focus on the more widely acknowledged areas of discrimination such as maternity, race and religion; therefore, expanding such training to encompass the discrimination and mistreatment of caregiving fathers is considered to be a positive step towards the minimisation of the 'fatherhood forfeits' as observed in this book. To maximise the success of such training, it is believed that it should incorporate elements of 'perspective taking' (Paluck et al., 2021) to enable participants to envision themselves in the shoes of the caregiving fathers, thus broadening the scope of more traditional methods of unconscious bias training (Gifford, 2021). Training in this area is important for both staff and managers, as advocated by Adrienne Burgess, Joint Chief Executive of the Fatherhood Institute, who states that it is critical that organisations are "equipping managers and the workforce to understand and address unconscious bias against men's caretaking that stigmatises those who seek to balance care for their children with the joys and demands of paid work" (Burgess, 2021b).

Fatherhood Forums

The final way that organisations can address the challenges posed by the 'fatherhood forfeits' identified in this book is through the establishment of fatherhood forums. Fatherhood forums can create a sense of community for fathers within the workplace, providing a space in which to discuss their concerns regarding caregiving and balancing work-family demands, share common challenges and explore ways to overcome them (Harrington et al., 2017). For example, the National Grid utilise social media and a corporate Yammer site as a mechanism by which fathers can share stories, ask questions and divulge hints and tips on a wide range of fatherhood issues (Working Families, Best Practice Awards, 2015). Through such forums fathers can address personal experiences of the challenges they face as fathers, which could be expanded to include specific discussions of any exposure to the 'fatherhood forfeits' with the purpose of raising awareness and taking action against the forfeits. Such discussion could be initiated through use of guest speakers to elicit wider exploration within the group (Harrington et al., 2017). PwC regularly engage speakers within their Parents and Carers network to explore the challenges and opportunities for parents in the workplace. They also have found that the sharing of online stories and videos is a helpful tool in this process (PwC, 2021).

Elliot Rae, author of "Dad" and founder of website 'Music, Football and Fatherhood' (https://musicfootballfatherhood.com), observes that such forums are "essential in supporting dads and helping them meet other men who are experiencing similar issues while also offering a space to celebrate and share parenting wins" (Rae, 2021). Thus, they can be conceptualised as specifically addressing the 'fatherhood forfeit' of 'struggling with friendships' through creating an opportunity for friendships to develop.

Often fatherhood forums are run by fathers themselves and supported by HR; such is the case within Scottish Parliament (Working Families, Best Practice Awards, 2021). Naturally, for smaller organisations, arranging a forum is more challenging. Thus, it has been suggested that in this scenario, smaller firms might engage with external online parenting groups, such as Music Fatherhood and Football (www.musicfootballfatherhood.com), and could encourage their staff to engage with this mechanism (Forbes & Birkett, 2020).

Some organisations opt for a broader approach, such as Nestle's Parent Talk network which is open to both mothers and fathers; however, to maximise the success of forums which are open to both parents, it is suggested that men need to be specifically encouraged to engage with them, and such extra effort pays dividends in the male numbers that join (Adams, 2021b).

With the recommended organisational actions to minimise the 'fatherhood forfeits' detailed, the final section of this book explores the potential actions at a macro level that can be taken minimise such forfeits in a broader sense.

GOVERNMENT ACTIONS FROM THE FATHERHOOD FORFEIT STUDY

At the macro level, it is suggested that changes to government policy have potential to reduce the impact of the 'fatherhood forfeits' as identified within in this book.

Firstly, this could include changes in government policy, such as giving fathers increased rights and access to leave that complements Shared Parental Leave, but that is independent of mothers and is funded nationally. Such a move by government to equalise leave provision on a nationwide level is likely to have a direct impact on the 'fatherhood forfeit' of 'obtaining less workplace support for caregiving than mothers', as well as reducing the challenges associated with 'Think Child–Think Mum' judgements. In addition, an equalisation of government policy regarding parental leave provisions might encourage eventual changes to the gender norms surrounding paternal behaviour and altering the landscape of 'social mistreatment'.

Secondly, government intervention could assist in the reduction of the 'fatherhood forfeits' through revisions of the Equality Act (2010). Currently, in relation to the family sphere within the Equality Act, only pregnancy and maternity are defined as protected characteristics. It is suggested that the addition of 'parental status' as a characteristic would ensure that fathers have protected legal rights rather than facing variable levels of 'good practice' across all job sectors. It is envisaged that this would specifically assist in the reduction of the 'fatherhood forfeits' of social mistreatment and the quantitative findings which found that when a father applicant applied for a part-time role they were less likely to be successful than a female applicant. Changing the legislation in this way would give fathers (and mothers) legal recourse if they felt they were subjected to mistreatment or did not secure a job or promotion due to their caregiving responsibilities.

Thirdly, it is suggested that an amendment is made to the Flexible Working Regulations (2014, within the Employment Rights Act, 1996).

As it currently stands in UK legislation, employees legally have the right to request flexible working; however, requests can be rejected fairly providing there is a 'valid business reason'. It is recommended that the legislation is modified so that all jobs are accepted as flexible automatically and if employers believe that the role cannot be undertaken flexibly they will need to demonstrate that there is a 'genuine occupational requirement' for this. The notion of 'genuine occupational requirements' is adopted within the Equality Act and goes further than the existing requirement of a 'valid business reason'. Such a change shifts responsibility away from the requirement for organisations to define a reason for rejection towards a climate where they needed to explicitly state why flexible working wasn't possible at the outset. It is believed that such a move would address the forfeit that 'fathers receive less organisational support for caregiving than mothers'.

The final action recommended for government as a way of reducing the 'fatherhood forfeits' is related to wider, compulsory reporting of the uptake rates of working arrangements that support caregiving through an Annual Flexibility Audit, akin to Gender Pay Gap Reporting. It is proposed that the reporting of working arrangements such as part-time working or flexible working might illuminate the disparities in workplace support with a view to minimising the 'fatherhood forfeits' as highlighted in this book, specifically the forfeit that 'fathers receive less organisational support for caregiving than mothers'. The Annual Flexibility Audit would require employers to map all roles within organisations, identifying the specific ways in which each role can be flexible and for this to be defined at the point of advertisement/shared with existing post holders with a view to increasing the gender neutrality of flexible work.

Chapter Summary and Recommendations

This book has explored in detail the workplace experiences of caregiving fathers and identified this grouping as facing 'fatherhood forfeits'. It has been demonstrated that caregiving fathers in the workplace face numerous challenges when they attempt to take an active role in the caregiving of their children. The findings of the 'Fatherhood Forfeit Study' can be categorised under four main types of 'Fatherhood Forfeit':

- Fathers are less likely to obtain a role that allows them to combine caregiving and work (such as part-time employment) due to scoring lower than their counterparts during the selection process.
- Caregiving fathers are considered as secondary parents due to 'Think Child–Think Mum' assumptions.
- Caregiving fathers 'Obtain less workplace support for caregiving than mothers'.
- Caregiving fathers face 'social mistreatment' which was identified as comprising facing 'mockery', being 'viewed as idle', 'struggling with friendships', facing 'negative judgement' and being viewed with 'suspicion'.

Limitations and Further Research

Overall, the findings of this study expand existing knowledge regarding the workplace treatment of caregiving fathers through identifying the specific 'fatherhood forfeits' that caregiving fathers face in a UK context. However, it is important to acknowledge the limitations of this study and to signpost potential future areas for research. The sample for this study was narrow, primarily due to the predominance of married, heterosexual, white British participants who came forward as participants. Whilst this is the most prevalent family type in the UK and a lack of diversity is a common critique of research in this area, it is not known to what extent these findings would differ if the sample was more varied (ONS, 2020; Kelliher et al., 2019; Li et al., 2018). Therefore, it is suggested that further research is undertaken with a larger, stratified sample to encompass more diversity in ethnicity and family composition, thus representing contemporary UK society more adequately. Additionally, the study reported within this book is UK specific, and the broad concept of the 'fatherhood forfeit' that emerged in this context warrants wider exploration to consider whether it also emerges in contemporary international contexts, and if so, the extent to which it acts as a barrier to fathers caregiving activities.

It has been highlighted in this chapter that the Covid-19 pandemic has brought with it much promise regarding potential changes to societal norms surrounding parenting. It is expected that the post-pandemic employment landscape will be typified by a more flexible employment model, and organisational and government actions have been suggested to capitalise on this potential change and to directly address the 'fatherhood forfeits'. Specifically, it has been highlighted that experiences during the pandemic might result in a reduction of some of the workplace barriers surrounding access to paid leave and inability to work from home which are often cited as key impediments to fathers' involvement in caregiving (Carlson et al., 2020; Lenhart et al., 2019). Thus, capitalisation upon the societal shifts that appear to have occurred during this period are likely to be a key feature in organisational recovery from the Covid-19 pandemic. However, it is important to note that this is not without complexity, as illustrated by Sarah Jackson, OBE:

> Tackling the 'fatherhood forfeits' may pose a bigger challenge than the mummy track because it is so counter-cultural for men to step away from the breadwinner role and embrace active, visible fatherhood. There are unconscious and as well as open biases in play, that combine to discourage fathers from challenging the expected path. (Jackson, 2021)

Thus, a multi-action approach is suggested, incorporating as many of the outlined actions as is practical, with emphasis placed on increasing understanding of the 'fatherhood forfeits' to reduce and eventually eradicate them. To enable this, key recommendations have been made at both the organisational and the government levels.

Key Recommendations for Reducing Fatherhood Forfeits in the Workplace

At the Organisational Level

- Equalise organisational policy and leave arrangements between mothers and fathers.
- Specific manager training on the management of flexible working requests from fathers and how to support fathers in the workplace.
- Establish clear policies in relation to flexible working and ensure they are promoted internally, with gender neutrality inherent and senior management role modelling them.
- Consider advertising all roles as flexible from the outset.
- Review bullying and harassment policies to ensure that there is a zero-tolerance policy on the 'Social Mistreatment of Caregiving Fathers'.

- Organisational training for all staff that specifically addresses the mistreatment of caregiving fathers—this may include expansion of any existing unconscious bias training to include the mistreatment of caregiving fathers as a grouping.
- Establish mentoring schemes for fathers.
- Establish a fatherhood forum.
- Ongoing monitoring of interventions and making appropriate adjustments.

At the Government Level

- An increase of rights for fathers for paid leave, independent of mothers, to complement Shared Parental Leave.
- Revision of the list of protected characteristics within the Equality Act (2010) to include 'parental status', to give caregiving fathers protected legal rights.
- Amendment to the Flexible Working Regulations (2014) to establish that all job roles are flexible by default and that any deviation from this requires identification of a 'Genuine Occupational Requirement'.
- Introduction of a compulsory Annual Flexibility Audit.

REFERENCES

Adams, J. (2021a, July 14). *Via email with Jasmine Kelland.*
Adams, J. (2021b). *Daddy jobs' (2021).* Available at: https://daddyjobs.co.uk/category/shared-parental-leave. Accessed 12 Nov 2021.
Alon, T., Doepke, M., Olmstead-Rumsey, J., & Tertilt, M. (2020). The impact of Covid-19 on gender equality. *Covid Economics: Vetted and Real-Time Papers, 4,* 62–85.
Andrew, A., Cattan, S., Costa Dias, M., Farquharson, C., Kraftman, L., Krutikova, S., & Sevilla, A. (2020, May). *How are mothers and fathers balancing work and family under lockdown?* (IFS Briefing Note BN290). Institute for Fiscal Studies. https://www.ifs.org.uk/uploads/BN290-Mothers-and-fathers-balancing-work-and-life-under-lockdown.pdf
APLEN. (2019). *National Working Families Report, Advancing Parental Leave Equality network.* Available at: https://aplen.pages.ontraport.net/WorkingFamiliesReport2019. Accessed 12 Nov 2021.
Aviva. (2021). Available at: https://www.aviva.com/newsroom/news-releases/2021/07/gender-divisions-in-work-life-beyond-the-pandemic/. Accessed 12 Nov 2021.

Burgess, A. (2021a). *Lockdown fathers- the untold story.* Fatherhood Institute.

Burgess, A. (2021b, July 14). *Via email with Jasmine Kelland.*

Burrell, S. R., & Ruxton, S. (2020). *The impact of the Covid-19 crisis on work with men and boys in Europe.* Durham University.

Carlson, D. L., Petts, R. J., & Pepin, J. R.. (2020). *Men and women agree: During the COVID-19 pandemic men are doing more at home. They differ over how much, but in most households the division of housework and childcare has become more equal* (Council on Contemporary Families Briefing Paper, 20).

Chung, H., & Van der Horst, M. (2020). Flexible working and unpaid overtime in the UK: The role of gender, parental and occupational status. *Social Indicators Research, 151*(2), 495–520.

Chung, H., Birkett, H., Forbes, S., & Seo, H. (2020). *Working from home and the division of housework and childcare among dual earner couples during the pandemic in the UK.* https://www.birmingham.ac.uk/Documents/college-social-sciences/business/research/wirc/epp-working-from-home-COVID-19-lockdown.pdf

Cito, G., Micelli, E., Cocci, A., Polloni, G., Coccia, M. E., Carini, M., Minervini, A., & Natali, A. (2020). Paternal behaviors in the era of COVID-19. *The World Journal of Men's Health, 38*(3), 251.

Dinwiddy, I. (2021, July 20). *Via email with Jasmine Kelland.*

Forbes and Birkett. (2020). *Fatherhood toolkit.* Available at: https://more.bham.ac.uk/fathersintheworkplace/fathers-in-the-workplace-toolkit-for-smes/policies-for-smes/. Accessed 12 Nov 2021.

Forbes, L. K., Lamar, M. R., Speciale, M., & Donovan, C. (2021). Mothers' and fathers' parenting attitudes during COVID-19. *Current Psychology,* 1–10.

Gifford, J. (2021). *Unconscious bias training is not the go-to solution.* Available at: https://www.cipd.co.uk/Community/blogs/b/jonny_gifford/posts/unconscious-bias-training-is-not-the-go-to-solution?CommentSortBy=CreatedDate&CommentSortOrder=Descending

Government Equalities Office. (2020). *What motivates employers to improve their Shared Parental Leave and pay offers?* Research report prepared by Sarah Forbes, Holly Birkett and Penny Smith. https://assets.publishing.service.gov.uk/government/uploads/system/uploads/attachment_data/file/952934/What_motivates_employers_to_improve_their_Shared_Parental_Leave_and_pay_offers.pdf

Harrington, B., Van Deusen, F., & Fraone, J. S. (2017). *The new dad: The career-caregiving conflict.* Boston College Center for Work & Family. Available at: https://www.bc.edu/content/dam/files/centers/cwf/research/publications/researchreports/BCCWF%20The%20New%20Dad%202017

Henz, U. (2017). *Father involvement in the UK: Trends in the new millennium* (Families and Societies Working Paper 70). Available from http://www.familiesandsocieties.eu/wp-content/uploads/2017/02/WP70Henz2017.pdf. Accessed 27 Oct 2020.

Jackson, S. (2021, July 20). *Via email with Jasmine Kelland.*

Kelland, J., Radcliffe, L., & Gregory Chialton, J. (2020). *Written Evidence (LBC0090): Submission to the Select Committee on the impact of Covid.* University of Plymouth. https://committees.parliament.uk/writtenevidence/9853/html/

Kelliher, C., Richardson, J., & Boiarintseva, G. (2019). All of work? All of life? Reconceptualising work-life balance for the 21st century. *Human Resource Management Journal, 29*(2), 97–112.

King, T., Hewitt, B., Crammond, B., Sutherland, G., Maheen, H., & Kavanagh, A. (2020). Reordering gender systems: Can COVID-19 lead to improved gender equality and health? *The Lancet, 396*(10244), 80–81.

Langner, L. A. (2018). Flexible men and successful women: The effects of flexible working hours on German couples' wages. *Work, Employment and Society, 32*(4), 687–706.

Lenhart, A., Swenson, H., & Schulte, B. (2019). *Lifting the barriers to paid family and medical leave for men in the United States.* The New America Report.

Li, A., Butler, A., & Bagger, J. (2018). Depletion or expansion? Understanding the effects of support policy use on employee work and family outcomes. *Human Resource Management Journal, 28*(2), 216–234.

Mangiavacchi, L., Piccoli, L., & Pieroni, L. (2021). Fathers matter: Intrahousehold responsibilities and children's wellbeing during the COVID-19 lockdown in Italy. *Economics & Human Biology, 42,* 101016.

Mihalich-Levin, L. (2021, July 15). *Via email with Jasmine Kelland.*

Nestle. (2021). https://www.nestle.co.uk/en-gb/media/news/it-easy-be-parent-uk

Office of National Statistics. (2020). *Coronavirus and employment for parents in the UK;* October to December 2019. https://www.ons.gov.uk/peoplepopulationandcommunity/healthandsocialcare/conditionsanddiseases/articles/coronavirusandemploymentforparentsintheuk/octobertodecember2019. Accessed 12 Nov 2021.

Paluck, E. L., et al. (2021). Prejudice reduction: Progress and challenges. *Annual Review of Psychology, 72*(1), 533–560. New systematic review reviewed here https://www.cipd.co.uk/news-views/nutshell/issue-105/reducing-workplace-prejudice

PwC. (2021, November 11). *Via email with Jasmine Kelland.*

Rae, E. (2021, July 14). *Via email with Jasmine Kelland.*

Sevilla, A., & Smith, S. (2020). *Baby steps: The gender division of childcare during the COVID19 pandemic.* IZA DP IZA Institute of Labor Economics. https://www.iza.org/publications/dp/13302/baby-steps-the-gender-division-of-childcare-during-the-covid-19-pandemic

Shafer, K., Scheibling, C., & Milkie, M. A. (2020). The Division of Domestic Labor before and during the COVID-19 Pandemic in Canada: Stagnation versus Shifts in Fathers', Contributions. *Canadian Review of Sociology/Revue canadienne de sociologie, 57*(4), 523–549.

The Guardian. (2021, June 10). *John Lewis to offer equal parental leave to all staff.* https://www.theguardian.com/business/2021/jun/10/john-lewis-to-offer-equal-parental-leave-to-all-staff#:~:text=The%20employee%2Downed%20retailer%2C%20which,leave%20scheme%20is%20%E2%80%9Cfailing%E2%80%9D

van Zyl, J (2021, August 2). *Via email with Jasmine Kelland.*

Whitley, C. (2021, July 13). *Via email with Jasmine Kelland.*

Working Families. (2015). *Best practice awards.* Available at: https://working-families.org.uk/employers/case-studies/national-grid-finalist-2015-the-cityfathers-best-for-all-stages-of-fatherhood-award/. Accessed 12 Nov 2021.

Working Families. (2020). *Best practice awards.* Available at: https://working-families.org.uk/employers/bestpracticeawards/2020-best-practice-awards-winners/. Accessed 12 Nov 2021.

Working Families. (2021). *Best practice awards.* Available at: htts://workingfamilies.org.uk/news/finalists-best-practice-awards-2021/. Accessed 12 Nov 2021.

AUTHOR INDEX

SUBJECT INDEX

© The Author(s), under exclusive license to Springer Nature   125
Switzerland AG 2022
J. Kelland, *Caregiving Fathers in the Workplace*,
https://doi.org/10.1007/978-3-030-97971-3